Preservation Politics

ABOUT THE SERIES
The American Association for State and Local History Book Series publishes technical and professional information for those who practice and support history, and addresses issues critical to the field of state and local history. To submit a proposal or manuscript to the series, please request proposal guidelines from AASLH headquarters: AASLH Book Series, 1717 Church St., Nashville, Tennessee 37203. Telephone: (615) 320-3203. Fax: (615) 327-9013. Website: www.aaslh.org.

ABOUT THE ORGANIZATION
The American Association for State and Local History (AASLH), a national history organization headquartered in Nashville, TN, provides leadership, service, and support for its members, who preserve and interpret state and local history in order to make the past more meaningful in American society. AASLH is a membership association representing history organizations and the professionals who work in them. AASLH members are leaders in preserving, researching, and interpreting traces of the American past to connect the people, thoughts, and events of yesterday with the creative memories and abiding concerns of people, communities, and our nation today. In addition to sponsorship of this book series, the Association publishes the periodical *History News*, a newsletter, technical leaflets and reports, and other materials; confers prizes and awards in recognition of outstanding achievement in the field; and supports a broad education program and other activities designed to help members work more effectively. To join the organization, go to www.aaslh.org or contact Membership Services, AASLH, 1717 Church St., Nashville, TN 37203.

Preservation Politics

Keeping Historic Districts Vital

WILLIAM E. SCHMICKLE

A division of
ROWMAN & LITTLEFIELD PUBLISHERS, INC.
Lanham • New York • Toronto • Plymouth, UK

Published by AltaMira Press
A division of Rowman & Littlefield Publishers, Inc.
A wholly owned subsidiary of The Rowman & Littlefield Publishing Group, Inc.
4501 Forbes Boulevard, Suite 200, Lanham, Maryland 20706
www.rowman.com

10 Thornbury Road, Plymouth PL6 7PP, United Kingdom

British Library Cataloguing in Publication Information Available

Library of Congress Cataloging-in-Publication Data
Schmickle, William Edgar, 1946–
  Preservation politics : keeping historic districts vital / William E. Schmickle.
    p. cm. — (American Association for State and Local History book series)
  Includes bibliographical references and index.
  ISBN 978-0-7591-2051-8 (cloth : alk. paper) — ISBN 978-0-7591-2052-5
(paper : alk. paper) — ISBN 978-0-7591-2053-2 (electronic)
  1. Historic districts—Conservation and restoration—United States.
2. Historic preservation—Political aspects—United States. 3. Historic
preservation—Government policy—United States. 4. United States—Cultural
policy. I. Title.
  E159.S36 2012
  973—dc23   2011050132

∞™ The paper used in this publication meets the minimum requirements of
American National Standard for Information Sciences—Permanence of Paper
for Printed Library Materials, ANSI/NISO Z39.48-1992.

Printed in the United States of America

Contents

CONTENTS

Preservation and the Politics of Change

I didn't go into politics to be loved, and I haven't been disappointed.

—Sen. Phil Graham

Have you and I met?

Perhaps you've read my first book, *The Politics of Historic Districts: A Primer for Grassroots Preservation.*[1] That was where I showed you, step by step, how to think and act politically to win a campaign for historic district designation.

By now, I guess, with or without my help, you have your district and **historic preservation commission (HPC)** up and running. Good.

So tell me: what's the most important heritage resource you'd like to see survive? Is it some streetscape or iconic building? Really? Isn't it your **district institutions**: your ordinance, HPC, design guidelines, and procedures?

It's hard to say how many of our 2,500 historic districts will see this century out with their HPCs intact, but we know they're under stress. Property values have plummeted, public coffers are emptying, history tourism has tumbled, and antigovernment feeling is entrenched and deepening.

Perhaps that's all passing. But then there is *the* question we've been facing all along. There are many ways to phrase it. Let me share the one that put me on this path.

THE QUESTION

"Why don't they love us more?" the HPC commissioner asked from the floor at the 2002 NAPC Forum in San Antonio. These biennial meetings of the National Alliance of Preservation Commissions offer an unparalleled chance to network, learn, celebrate—and commiserate about community attitudes.

I felt for her naïveté. Folks don't ever really love government, do they? Especially not regulatory commissions. So I piped up with Henry Kissinger's quip about why women found him irresistible. "Power," he deadpanned, "is the ultimate aphrodisiac."

I said we might be more attractive, too, if we used the power of our HPCs more effectively. Pointing out that power is the currency of politics, I said that unfortunately we preservationists have tended to shun politics. The voices saying "Yeah" and "What about it?" told me that I was onto something.

Have you, too, noticed a collective disdain of politics among our preservation colleagues? Politics is what others do—not us!—to game the decision-making process. To hear some tell it, politics is all backroom arm twisting and deal cutting, payoffs and paybacks. "Keep politics and connections out of preservation," reads the lead-in to one Philadelphia news story.[2]

Of course politics stinks sometimes. In Tombstone, Arizona, preservation has been characterized by "what locals describe as 'nasty' political infighting."[3]

More commonly, politics is just the routine way public life is carried on. Results layer up so slowly that the process may pass unnoticed. That's how most change happens.

So what do you think? Is a basic resistance to change behind our suspicion of politics?

POLITICS AND CHANGE

We preservationists like to say we're not opposed to change. Yet we often don't seem to know what to do with change except to try to rope it off or beat it into submission.

Our gut instinct tells us that folks who don't share our priorities use politics to change things on us. And so we identify politics with developers, for instance, whose projects threaten **historic resources**. We routinely decry *politics* when we really mean to deny all of them *options*.

Consider this example. In Madison, Wisconsin, a development company figured out how to get the Common [City] Council to overturn the denial of a hotel project by the Historic Landmarks Commission (one of many names for HPCs). Critic Jason Tish later concluded that this established "a model for gaining approval for a project that would otherwise not be allowed by existing zoning regulations." As he described it in his blog: "Sell the project to city officials, and as many Council members, neighbors, and members of the public as will buy it, and the codified zoning restrictions, including Historic District requirements, are up for negotiation."[4]

I have to ask: what's wrong with that? Isn't it *exactly* how most of us got our districts designated? Did we really think we could slam the door on politics and lock it, much less give up politics ourselves?

CHANGING POLITICS

Because designation didn't banish politics, we might get it in our heads to change the way it works. Most of us would like to see politics be more predictable and deliberate than it actually is, less haphazard and up for grabs. We'd much prefer a political world driven by values and reason than by interests and influence equals power, as Kissinger put it.

When David Grinnell writes to the *Washington Post* opposing overhead wires for new streetcars in the District of Columbia's historic core, he cites an 1889 law prohibiting overhead electrification as having given "us a city of sweeping vistas, open sky and sun-filled streets." So he calls on all parties, "Let us reason together as citizens . . . which is a privilege and responsibility as well as a joy."[5]

I sympathize with him, don't you? He calls upon our better angels. His optimism flatters us. He actually seems to think it's possible for us to submit all our competing interests to the independent arbiter of reason.

But to what end? Does it sound to you like he expects reasoning to produce any result other than one congenial to his view? His call to reason has all the circular appeal of a noose.

Open politics—which is normal politics as we experience it—begins with contending interests and moves forward toward some as-yet-to-be-determined end. Many of us, however, prefer to reason backward, starting with a principled or legal case for what we want and carving away incompatible interests along the way.

Shoot, who could resist doing that?

Not Meg Maguire of the Committee of 100 on the Federal City, which Grinnell once chaired. She flatly told a *Post* reporter that Washington's cherished vistas are "not to be tampered with." Period. Their allies include the National Park Service and the Capital Planning Commission.

On the other side, D.C. transportation chief Gabe Klein argues, "You have to weigh the impact of a single overhead wire . . . versus the importance of connecting residents, businesses and visitors with needed jobs and services."

The stakes are high, with a historic legacy on one side and on the other what the *Post* describes as the "next catalyst of [the city's] rebirth," this effort "to bring back Washington's still languishing neighborhoods."

Klein is said to be floating a compromise even as rails are being laid and a few cars purchased. But City Council member Tommy Wells has heard enough. As I write, he's ready to introduce a bill to overturn the 1889 law and, as reported, "upend the definition of downtown Washington held for more than two centuries." He would have the Council determine what viewsheds are worthy of protection.

What do you say to that? "Politics!"—right? Of course. But whose?

Here's what Wells thinks: "The [preservation] purists are making this a religion rather than a practicality. . . . If the National Park Service only sees themselves as the steward of what happened over 120 years [ago], we've got a problem."[6]

He says "we've got a problem," but it's *their* problem, not his. What he's saying between the lines is that they're taking themselves out of serious political contention by shutting out other interests from the get-go.

A POLITICAL LESSON

The moral is straightforward. When we confront politics as it is with a preferred notion of how it ought to work, we don't change politics. We only kid ourselves and diminish our influence.

That said, it might just be that what we're witnessing in Washington are just opening gambits, a setting out of markers, shots across the bow, that sort of thing. Or perhaps that's what they'll become after experience teaches its hard lessons, and we can look back with the 20/20 vision of hindsight.

The danger is that we often seduce ourselves into error with the attractiveness of preferred ways of thinking. This isn't to say values are unimportant and reason has no role to play. And don't misread me: I'm not passing judgment on the merits of the issues. But if what we want is good for our communities, then we have a moral responsibility to succeed.

Being right—or having that confidence—helps. But politics does not reward good intentions that get in the way of a clear appreciation of the practical requirements of successful action.

Do you see what I'm getting at? The proper treatment for how we feel when politics provokes us is not less politics or different politics, but more politics, better done.

We waste far too much energy gnashing our teeth and dealing *with* politics. In the midst of a Boise district fight, Sonja Nehr-Kent says, "We need to get the politics under control and do what's best for our future."[7] But what we actually need to do is learn to work *within* politics, taking it for what it really is: the way civil society handles conflict and change.

WORKING WITHIN POLITICS

All government is institutionalized politics. That includes HPCs as governmental agencies. We didn't fight for designation to put an end to the politics of competing interests, but to sluice it into channels framed by **law**.

Back then we had a common enemy: defeat. And now? We have a common cause: delivering good government, which too often seems little understood.

I've sat through many HPC training sessions. What I've often missed is some deeper understanding of public service beyond instruction in best practices. Without a grasp of civic purpose, the best technique can come a cropper.

So what's the problem? Most of us who serve on HPCs are new to public service. We come on board for preservation, and then we err by taking dead aim at using our law and procedures for defending heritage resources against competing interests.

James Madison—the best practical political thinker our nation has produced—set us straight in *Federalist* 62: "A *good government* implies two things: first, fidelity to the object of government, which is the happiness of the people; secondly, a knowledge of the means by which that object can be best attained."

What does that say to us? Historic districts should put smiles on people's faces. Our task as public servants is to weave the community's interest in preservation among contending interests others see as good.

Under the project guidance of James K. Reap, the NAPC has produced a *Code of Ethics for Commissioners and Staff* that defines our charge. The preamble states: "The ethical [HPC] commissioner or staff member must carefully balance various public and private interests based on the facts and context of each situation guided by the commitment to serve the public interest."[8]

Doing this isn't rocket science. In some respects it's harder. We have no certain formulas, and the trajectories of our decisions are more difficult to plot. Then sometimes, too, they blow up in our faces.

THINKING BIG

Every week brings new reports of attacks upon our districts. When we fend them off, we take it as a triumph. Unfortunately, as political columnist Matt Miller observes, averting catastrophe has become a measure of success in contemporary politics. It gives us "a shrunken sense of collective possibilities" while showing "how far we are from using politics to solve major problems."[9]

Defending our law-based prerogatives against assault is no sound strategy for our aging districts. It won't help us win over new generations to a culture of compliance. I like what Miller says: "The smallness of our politics doesn't match the size of our challenges."[10]

We need to think big politcally to live up to the promise of our districts.

WHO ARE YOU?

This "we" includes you, too, no matter what you do for preservation, privately or publicly, alone or in partnerships with others. The politics of HPCs concern us all, indivisibly. We knew this when we sought our district designations. Regardless of our own interests, we fought as one to keep the past within our living futures.

The worst thing in politics is to be right and lose. The second worst is to have won, and then to fritter away our victory through political neglect.

NOTES

1. William E. Schmickle, *The Politics of Historic Districts: A Primer for Grassroots Preservation* (Lanham, MD: AltaMira Press, 2007).

2. Amy L. Webb, "A Jury of Peers," *Philadelphia City Paper*, March 18–24, 2004, at www.citypaper.net.

3. Susan Carroll, "Old West to Faux West," *Arizona Republic*, September 7, 2005, at www.azcentral.com.

4. Jason Tish, "Edgewater: Losing the Preservation Argument," Executive Director's Blog, June 10, 2010, at www.madisonpreservation.org.

5. David Grinnell, letter, *Washington Post*, April 14, 2010.

6. Lisa Reih, "Streetcar Effort May Go Down to the Wire," *Washington Post*, April 6, 2010.

7. Emily Simnitt, "Boise OKs Historic District," *Idaho Statesman*, June 1, 2004, at www.idahostatesman.com.

8. National Alliance of Preservation Commissions, *Code of Ethics for Commissioners and Staff* (Athens, GA: Author).

9. Matt Miller, "Defining Democracy Down," *Washington Post*, July 8, 2011.

10. Miller, "Defining Democracy Down."

ONE

Glimpsing Our Political Future

> More know how to win than to make proper use of victory.
>
> —Polybius

Some years ago in North Carolina, I co-led the citizens' campaign to designate Oak Ridge as Guilford County's first rural historic district. That's when I became a preservationist.

We were under the gun. We were a small, unincorporated village and easy prey for the North Carolina Department of Transportation. The law was stacked against us. Zoning was no help. But we had learned that local designation might head off a plan to bisect our old tobacco-farming community with a superhighway.

Our opponents scoffed. They said we were already dividing the neighborhood with our proposal. Some were okay with the road, some not. They had other competing interests, too. The fight was terrible right up to the end.

Sound familiar? I'll bet your own historic district began in crisis. But expectations were broader than just beating back a threat, weren't they? You, or those who went before you, looked to a better, even easier future for your community. Perhaps you prayed, "Just get us through this fight."

When the County Commission handed us our victory on a narrow vote, there were hugs and backslaps all round. It was nighttime on the ride home, yet all I saw ahead were bright, sunlit uplands. Such was the flush of victory.

At a moment like that, no one wants to be reminded of Winston Churchill's timeless observation: "The problems of victory are more agreeable than those of defeat, but they are no less difficult."

THE CONTINUATION OF POLITICS

What happened next in Oak Ridge happens everywhere. If you were present at the creation of your district, then you already understand.

After victory, folks on all sides of the issue return to their self-absorbed everyday lives, grateful the neighborhood battle is over. Leaders who have won the vote retire from public life or shift gears as the work of protecting historic resources moves into the routine of HPC processes. Politics seems to evaporate, to be replaced by the more civilized business of administering the law.

The truth is that it doesn't. Law is the outcome of politics at any given time, reflecting the distribution of influence among competing parties when the vote is taken. But the establishment of new law itself doesn't adjourn politics.

Politics arises naturally anywhere, anytime interests come into conflict. Interests and conflicts among them, big and small, are constant features of all communities regardless of how the law stands. And those interests—preservation included—are always evolving, contending, and eroding previous settlements among them.

But then we know that. There was once zoning law, and we were agents of change in our community who campaigned to change the law.

If now we are to keep our law and make it work, we have to think politically—which means thinking in terms of competing interests that are the engine of constant change within our district. And so it is that our politics transits from the requirements of victory to those of sustaining what we've won.

A STARTLING DISCOVERY

That night, driving home, had I been looking into a crystal ball instead of through my windshield, would I have seen a future like the one I found when I later moved to Annapolis?

Annapolis, Maryland, the most beautiful coastal town between Charleston and New England. *National Geographic* has called it "Camelot on the Bay." John F. Kennedy even intervened to save a few historic blocks from an encroaching U.S. Naval Academy, itself a National Historic Landmark District. A stunningly original colonial seaport, Maryland's capital has so many outstanding properties as to make Williamsburg blush. Its three hundred years of architectural history have crowded a waterfront that is today the sailing capital of America. A visitor finds it easy to get out on the water, turn toward shore, and marvel at our soaring domes and spires.

Here I found the gold standard of local-historic district setups. The seven-member HPC and full-time preservation planner, plus assistant and consultants, oversaw a model ordinance now in its fifth decade. Nothing could be torn down or built or altered without a certificate of approval (**COA**). The only appeal was to Circuit Court.

It looked like a good place to invest a life. So after careers in academe and college health, my wife and I bought a Victorian bed and breakfast, Flag House Inn, and found all around us—what?

Pride of place, but also a shocking culture of complaint.

The first time I attended a meeting of our Ward One Residents Association, I saw the City's Chief of Historic Preservation and the HPC chair in the dock. I was reminded of the contentious community meetings we held during our designation campaign in Oak Ridge. Didn't these folks know what they had?

So I began talking to neighbors. I pointed out that nothing in town would be as good—or better—without the historic district. What I got back were "yes, buts." Some said the district had become what our opponents said ours would be in Oak Ridge: a layer of arbitrary, capricious, even stifling bureaucracy, by turns too effective in regulating choice and ineffective in overseeing changes.

I bided my time. Then I joined the HPC as a commissioner, soon becoming vice chair. The reality I found was a lot better than my neighbors suspected. But almost no one attended meetings much who didn't have to, despite the ease of walking to City Hall in our most-walkable historic district.

As I progressed toward the chairmanship, my predecessor ran crisp, professional meetings twice a month. A nip here, a tuck there, and almost every application got approved in timely fashion.

You'd think the word would have gotten out. But that's not human nature, is it?

An architect tells the story of how a major home addition fairly sailed through the HPC, save for a minor change to the original structure. "That went well," he said to his client afterward. "What do you mean?" came the reply. "Those SOBs denied my window!" You can guess what his friends heard and neighbors repeated.

Our practices weren't perfect. What I think of as the bookends of the approval process—**outreach education** and enforcement—were just about nonexistent throughout my tenure, despite earnest efforts. Owners bruised their properties with annoying regularity. Sometimes on the sly, sometimes out of ignorance. Too often their introduction to the historic district came through "Stop Work!" orders—and then not often enough.

The City itself seemed bent at times on sidestepping the HPC. A new mayor refused to submit for review a major public-works project at a key historic site. Not that her plan was controversial: it was easily approvable.

Though our ordinance prevailed on points, some City departments kept a different scorecard. Their attitude comforted shirkers everywhere.

What in the world had happened in the decades since designation? Surely this wasn't the future foreseen by St. Clair Wright, the legendary activist who "saved Annapolis."

I wondered: was something like this down the road for the friends I left behind in Oak Ridge?

EVERYWHERE IS POLITICALLY THE SAME

Annapolis is a constant inspiration. The town remains spectacular.

As I travel the country I've yet to find an aspect of preservation politics—positive or negative—that Annapolis doesn't in some way typify. Yes, every district is different. Each has its own set of personalities, its matrix of interests, and its problem complexities. Preservation itself looks different from place to place, too. Ordinances vary, as do the scope and details of the design guidelines used in reviewing applications for COAs.

Even so, all districts are politically the same. Insight into one is insight into them all. You Agatha Christie fans will know what I mean. Annapolis is for me what St. Mary Mead is to Miss Marple. No matter where she goes—even London—she sees the themes of her little village playing out again and again.

That's why we can benefit from each other's experiences and sleuth out solutions to our most common problems. Whatever our successes or failures, we succeed or fail for basically the same reasons.

OUR COMMON CRISIS

When preservationists get together, we often talk about our worst problems and nod with friendly understanding. But we're missing something, aren't we? Something more difficult to treat.

Anton Chekhov put our problem well: "Any idiot can face a crisis—it is day to day living that wears you out." Simply put, aging is our common crisis. Sooner or later it catches up with all our historic districts.

TWO

The Road to Crisis in Historic Districts

Life is a series of collisions with the future.

—Jose Ortega y Gassett

How old is your historic district? Five years, ten, twenty . . . older? No matter. We're all pilgrims on the same road.

So how's your district doing? Hard to say, isn't it? Should you call in some professionals for an evaluation? The National Trust for Historic Preservation or your own State Historic Preservation Office can help.

But wait a minute. Why not just ask those with a direct interest in your work—property owners, architects, contractors, and realtors, for example? Have them in for a chat, and bring in local preservationists.

Or do you worry about stirring up a hornets' nest?

All right, then, how do *you* think you're doing? Do you feel you're pretty good at decision making? Are you discharging

your responsibilities in accordance with your ordinance, procedures, and accepted practices? Do you take satisfaction from
doing the best you can? Do you leave HPC meetings humming
a happy tune?

Or are you just whistling past the graveyard?

IN MEMORIAM

City councils rarely disband districts, but they do. Is it that they
just "don't get preservation," as some say? Perhaps. But even
those who agree with us on issues may fail to back us in a crisis.

They understand that districts get established to help solve
local problems and deliver benefits. When we create more head-
aches than we're worth, they feel it's we who "don't get politics."

Politicians are creatures of interests for whom no position,
once taken, is ever final and no district, once established, is secure. The last decade has shown that the threat of repeal is real
if not pervasive.

- Residents of the Oliver Street Historic District in Owosso,
  Michigan, petitioned for and won repeal of their district.[1]
- Monterey, Virginia, repealed its historic district.[2]
- The Estes Park, Colorado, historic district never had a
  chance. Three months after designation, the Town Board
  responded to a citizen petition and repealed designation.[3]
- In Palo Alto, California, the City Council voted unani-
  mously to revoke its temporary preservation law following
  a public vote overturning a nearly identical law the previous month.[4]
- Some districts never draw a breath. A local preservationist told a workshop I conducted that their Sauk City,

Wisconsin, campaign for district designation "crashed and burned" so badly that the City Council rewrote the ordinance to prohibit historic districts.

As I write, the Utah state legislature has voted to put a moratorium on the authority of local governments to designate historic districts, as a direct result of the conflict over designating the Yalecrest neighborhood in Salt Lake City.[5]

THREATS

Other districts have come under threat from the sorts of folks who originally opposed their designation and have not been mollified by their administration.

- In Albuquerque, 51 percent of business owners in the Huning Highland Historic District were seeking in 2004 to have the district abolished in favor of a less-regulated conservation zone. Bill Hoch of the Historic District Association said if the effort was successful, "then all the other districts are going to face the same dissolution."[6]
- Preservationists in Manitou Springs, Colorado, turned back a campaign by local property owners to create a "Swiss cheese option," allowing them to opt out of the district.[7]
- A member of the City Council of Saugatuck, Michigan, circulated a petition to abolish the local historic district. He was a party in a dispute and had lost a court appeal.[8]
- In Hartford, Connecticut, the historic district, established in 1974, narrowly escaped repeal when a ballot fell just short of the 75 percent required for de-designation.[9]

Even when these efforts fail, one gets a feeling of districts living on the edge.

ROLLBACK

Elsewhere, we see city councils paring down the size of districts or trimming their authority.

- The Park City, Utah, City Council began considering a plan to streamline the approval process, eliminate the Historic District Commission, transfer some of its authority to the Planning Commission, and create a new HPC that would have no review authority. "I applaud this day," said local architect Peter Barnes.[10]
- Houston has made it harder to designate districts, requiring support by owners of 67 percent of all tracts in a district for approval, while setting at 10 percent the number needed to initiate repeal—which requires only 51 percent support. Alternatively, district boundaries may be shrunk till 67 percent of remaining properties register support.[11]
- The Town Council in Strasburg, Virginia, suspended the administration and enforcement of its local preservation ordinance after being "thrashed" by residents who said that its guidelines were too intrusive. The guidelines, as I write, are under review.[12]

What happened in Monte Sereno, California, is especially telling. The community "pulled the teeth of its own preservation ordinance by making preservation status on any home—regardless of its historic value—a homeowner option." This led to the mass resignation of the HPC's membership.[13]

OVERTURNING HPC DECISIONS

Overturning decisions on appeal is more common. When it happens, the effect on the HPC may be demoralizing.

One example should suffice. Rulings by the Fredericksburg, Virginia, City Council overturning two decisions of the Architectural Review Board led to resignations in 2005. "The City Council is not really interested in preserving the Historic District at this point in time," said ARB member John Sperlazza. "I've had enough."[14]

WARNING SIGNS

Repeal, rollback, and overturned decisions. Each represents a different type of crisis. But all have deeper antecedents in a changing climate of attitudes toward historic districts. Many of our districts have already seen rifts opening.

- In Frederick, Maryland, "long-standing contention" between the HPC and some city residents "resulted in numerous attacks" that threw up a roadblock against the designation of a new district.[15]
- Amy Skaggs in Oak Park, Illinois, spoke out with others to oppose the expansion of their historic district on the grounds that "whatever the process is right now, it is very difficult."[16]

Such signposts on the road to future crises are all around us today. As our districts age, we can't like our chances if we don't recognize and deal with these issues in time.

We all should be as serious about our community relationships as we are about historic buildings. Then we would see these examples as the cracks in the foundation of the public's trust in us.

TRUST

Trust is the most fragile commodity in politics. When we floated the idea of a historic district in Oak Ridge, some neighbors were aggrieved. They said that we didn't trust them with their properties. So they returned the favor. They claimed we shouldn't be trusted with the power of a HPC.

Of course, they were right. "The truth," said Madison, "is that all men having power ought to be mistrusted." And yet he knew someone has to govern.

In the end we won our neighbors' trust, and after that the vote. Their hard-won trust in us gave legitimacy to our district process.

We lose legitimacy when folks perceive that the district process isn't working as it should or producing acceptable results. Worst-case scenarios unfold when we're perceived as seizing the benefits of power for ourselves to protect what interests us.

Tight-fisted or ham-handed regulation makes little difference in how we are perceived in handling people's interests. Again in Frederick, Maryland, John Lockard says, "We're not anti-preservation, we're anti-HPC. Trying to deal with these folks is something more than you can bear."[17] Similarly, from Evansville, Indiana, we hear that "battle lines have been drawn between homeowners and the city's HPC."[18]

In Cheshire, Connecticut, Paul Johnson complained, "The people who have these homes [in the historic district] buy them because they want to maintain them. It's a matter," he said, "of trusting them to do what they'll say they will do."[19]

Property owners may feel beholden to the law yet not rightfully bound by us to do as we require. Connie Phipps liked the bumper sticker she saw in Colorado: "What will you do when the government owns you?" "That's the way I feel," she said in supporting the repeal of the Estes Park historic district.[20] Short of outright opposition, we may simply sense a thinning of community support in a gathering culture of complaint, indifference to the HPC, avoidance of our process, and evasion of the law.

The same goes for our relationship with other preservationists. They feel betrayed when we're ineffective in keeping community support for preservation.

Such abused expectations have a huge capacity for revenge. A district doesn't have to die to be judged moribund.

In a propreservation essay, writer Tom Wolfe has described New York City's Landmarks Preservation Commission (LPC) as a "defunct" board, "a bureau of the walking dead."[21] Andrew Jones has expressed his own frustration with the LPC from another angle. "They've made the process expensive for me," he said. "You begin to understand why some owners give up."[22]

Some go even further. "I'm really disappointed to say I'm even a member of this city," said a resident in Superior, Minnesota, in July, 2011. Critical of the Historic Preservation Advisory Committee's stand against a developer's plans to revive the downtown Palace Theater, she was "ready to sell my house and move out tomorrow."[23]

THE BREAK WITH THE COMMUNITY

A tragic commentary, isn't it, this break with neighbors? After all, local historic districts often are a community's signature civic achievement.

There is nothing more disheartening to former leaders of districting campaigns than watching folks turn against our HPCs. They can't help but wonder what it is *we've* forgotten that *they* once knew of politics.

NOTES

1. "Michigan County Libertarians Help Defeat Historic District Statute," November 2001, at www.lp.org.

2. L. M. Schwartz, "Precedent-Setting Victory for Property Rights: Local Historic District Abolished," September 8, 2004, at www.prfamerica.org.

3. Juley Harvey, "Repeal Granted: Town Board Votes to Repeal Historic District Ordinance; 3-3 Tie Broken by Mayor," *Estes Park (CO) Trail-Gazette*, June 16, 2011, at www.eptrail.com.

4. Marcella Bernhard, "Community: Preservation Ordinance Gone for Good," *Palo Alto (CA) Weekly*, April 26, 2000, at www.paloaltoonline.com.

5. Lisa Riley Roche, "Legislature OKs Yalecrest Historic District Moratorium," *Mojave Desert News*, March 8, 2011, at www.desertnews.com.

6. Rachel Alaimo-Monson, "Historic Districts May Lose Protection," *New Mexico Daily Lobo*, April 8, 2004, at www.dailylobo.com.

7. *Colorado Springs Gazette*, January 16, 2003; see also John Dicker, "Preservation or Coercion? Manitou's Historic District Polarizes Property Owners," *Colorado Springs Independent*, October 3, 2002, at www.csindy.com.

8. *Holland (MI) Sentinel*, April 12, 2011, at www.Hollandsentinel.com.

9. Vanessa de la Torre, "Town's Historic District Survives Special Election," *Hartford (CT) Courant*, September 27, 2007, at www.Courant.com.

10. Christopher Smart, "Historic District Panel Debated in Park City," *Salt Lake Tribune*, March 14, 2003.

11. "The Coming Historic District Repeal and Other Changes to Houston's Preservation Ordinance," October 13. 2010, at www.Swamplot.com.

12. Preston Knight, "After Outcry, Strasburg Puts Historic District Rules on Hold," *Northern Virginia Daily*, May 11, 2011, at www.nvdaily.com.

13. Editorial, *Los Gatos (CA) Weekly Times*, April 11, 2001, at www.svcn.com; Susan Anawalt, "'Voluntary' Ordinance Threatens Preservation," *Los Gatos (CA) Weekly Times*, April 27, 1997, at www.svcn.com.

14. Historic Fredericksburg Foundation newsletter, November–December 2005.

15. Erica L. Green, "Historic Preservation Commission Criticism Not Supported by Numbers," January 22, 2009, at www.gazette.net.

16. Jim Jaworski, "Residents Skeptical of New Historic District Boundaries," March 22, 2011, at www.triblocal.com.

17. Green, "Historic Preservation Commission Criticism Not Supported by Numbers."

18. Kristen Tucker and Sandra Hoy, "Price of Preservation," *Evansville Living*, March–April 2002, at www.evansvilleliving.com.

19. Luther Turmelle, "Just Three Turn Out in Cheshire to Hear Proposed Historic District Rule Changes," *New Haven Register*, February 8, 2011, at www.nhregister.com.

20. Harvey, "Repeal Granted."

21. Tom Wolfe, "The (Naked) City and the Undead," *New York Times*, November 26, 2006, at www.nytimes.com.

22. Alexandra Bandon, "The Landmarks Commission Approves Most Requests, but Some Homeowners Complain about Arbitrary Decisions," *New York Times*, December 5, 2004, at www.nytimes.com.

23. Richard Thomas, "Historic Restoration, Brick by Brick," July 3, 2011, at www.businessnorth.com.

THREE

Our District Designation Story

In our youth our hearts were touched with fire.

—Oliver Wendell Holmes, Jr.

I think it's a shame, really, that many preservationists have no background in the rough-and-tumble combat of a hard-fought campaign to establish a local historic district. It is an unforgettable, scorching experience for the politically unwary.

So I want to take you through a few basic features of such campaigns as though we were involved in one, ourselves. We can't cover everything here, not now. Just enough to get us squared away on common ground.[1]

We'll assume we have implacable opponents and a recalcitrant City Council. If your district had an easier time of it, then you likely will have missed important lessons for the future. They were always there in hiding, beneath the gloss of your good fortune. So listen up, for that's a shine that time will tarnish.

ADVOCACY AND POLITICS

Preservationists who are new to politics start districting campaigns at a distinct disadvantage. Instead of thinking politically, they like to think in terms of advocacy as persuasive education. They focus on framing a preservation message, getting it out, refining it, and sticking to it.

If you're a local activist and you ask for help in launching an advocacy campaign, you'll find lots of fine preservation folks at the local, state, and national levels ready to provide guidance. They'll help you master the precepts, law, and practices you'll need to make your case. And don't get me wrong: you have to do it.

So you study up and gain confidence. Your mentors are impressed. They come to see you as a capable advocate who is ready for public hearings. But if you end your preparations there, you can walk into a public meeting the best-informed party in the room, but the least prepared for the bare-knuckle fight you'll run into.

So let me clue you in.

The formal hearing process we go through down at City Hall is just that: a formality, right up to the vote. We can do absolutely everything right, get every approval we need as we work our way through advisory boards right up to the City Council, and still find our elected officials will do exactly as they please regardless of our arguments on behalf of preservation.

You see, the very idea of persuading anyone is far too rational and final for what actually happens. The City Council will listen to your points and take a head count of support and opposition. But what they really want to know is, *who* benefits, and where do *they* themselves fit in? Once they decide on that, they'll pick among the arguments they hear, pro and con, to justify their votes.

To budge them off square one, we need to show solid community support. The place to start is with recognizing that historic districting is intensely personal. It touches folks where they live, earn a living, raise their families, and invest their dreams.

We'll have to make our case to them as well as to the City Council. When we ask our neighbors for their help, we'll find that their responses are far more emotional and fluid, and less deliberative and decisive, than we might like.

People may agree with everything we say and yet refuse to back us. Or they might not care about preservation and still stand with us, for reasons of their own that may change from day to day.

Such cases aren't unknown to advocacy, but they are alien to its education focus. A mere handful of property owners going one way or the other can make or break our effort.

MISSING THE ISSUE

The problem with advocacy isn't simply that folks won't be much moved by education. It's that advocacy makes preservation the main issue in a districting campaign.

It isn't. When we talk to our neighbors, we'll find that most of them are already favorably inclined toward preservation, but only *up to a point*. Their support for *preservation* usually comes in at a point somewhere below a *historic district*. Here's the problem:

- You and I *think* "preservation" and *say* "historic district."
- They *hear* "historic district" and *think* "government regulation."

We don't have a *preservation* problem with them. We have a *districting* problem.

As we go on about preservation, our opponents will be crafting a strategy to exploit this difference. The contest is fully engaged when they declare: "This is a property-rights issue!" We argue the value, benefits, and merits of preservation. They hammer away on the merits, benefits, and value of property rights. Their strategy is a mirror image of our own, but with a difference. They don't have to justify themselves, put forward a counterproposal, or prove us wrong. All they have to do is stop us.

Advocacy finally falls apart for us when we realize this is no fair fight where issues are fought with reasoned arguments. Instead, it is a political contest for power in which our opponents use issues as weapons for gaining influence. Too often we wake up to our situation only as the wheel of politics runs over us. So let's go back and get a proper start before it is too late.

GOING TO THE COMMUNITY

Now that we're on the same page, we'll begin by accepting that there are actually two routes to district designation we should be going down.

- One is *required* by law and takes place at City Hall.
- The other is *advised* and located in the community.

The second route, which aims at winning the support of our neighbors, takes strategic precedence.

Once they know what we're about, folks will start picking sides. Our first political challenge is figuring out who's who.

Because districting is personal, the usual labels—such as *liberal* and *conservative*—go out the window. Everybody's tetchy when it comes to their own properties. They are either for us or against us—or, more likely at the start, undecided in the middle.

So we're looking at three fluid groupings. I call them Makers, Breakers, and Takers. (A fourth group—**Shapers**, such as the media—influences opinion from outside.)

- **Makers**—that's us—want to win designation and have the wherewithal to do it.
- **Breakers** are die-hard opponents determined to stop us.
- **Takers** are fence-sitters who could take the district or leave it and are making up their minds.

Now think of a seesaw with fairly small clusters of committed Makers and Breakers at either end. Takers—by far the largest group—occupy the space between them. Our task is to end up with the mass of Takers on our side. In the seesaw metaphor, whoever ends up with feet firmly on the ground wins.

PRESERVATION-PLUS

So how do we do it? Advocacy tries to bring folks to *our* side by persuading them we're right. The way we win is by getting them to see we're on *their* side and support *their* interests.

Get it? We push the seesaw's fulcrum as far toward the Breakers as possible, inclining the majority our way while our opponents are left dangling in the air.

To gain the weight of the vital center on our side, we don't start by telling folks what interests *us* about the past and preservation. We talk about what interests *them* as they think about their futures. Is it economic security? Commercial revitalization? A stronger voice at City Hall? Influencing public works? Keeping a well-worn school in the neighborhood? Stopping teardowns and McMansions? Saving a church? Strengthening community? Or is it as simple as folks wanting to protect their own investments against despoiling neighbors?

We inquire to lead. We listen so we may think. We're not trying to be all things to all people, just many things to many people. That's how politics is played. Then we use what we've learned to shape a practical vision of a changing community in which preservation plays an important role.

This winning strategy is what I call **preservation-plus**. It isn't a substitute for preservation advocacy. It's a strategic adjustment for forging a consensus for districting within a community in conflict over our proposal. It entails roping in allies and reinforcements across the broadest possible spectrum of interests.

Our goal is to create the objective conditions of our political success, shifting attention from regulation to big-picture possibilities, without downplaying regulation. We forthrightly admit that the district will put a regulatory squeeze on all of us. But preservation-plus is designed to demonstrate what my Oak Ridge friend Frank Whitaker phrased so aptly: "the juice is worth the squeeze."

WINNING AT CITY HALL

We pursue this community strategy even as we are going through the formal approval process down at City Hall. Then we take what we've won in the community to the City Council for the vote.

With community support in hand, we are able to change the question of the hour. Instead of asking the Council to vote on designation, we challenge them to vote for what our community has already decided on its own.

We expect that some of our neighborhood opponents will stand on *property rights*. Well, we'll say we believe in them, too. But—and here's the difference—we also hold fast to our *political rights* as citizens to come together to decide to do good things for our community and to see that laws and institutions are created equal to the task.

If the City Council balks at imposing the district on those who stand against us, we'll tell them something they already know: that no matter what the issue is, some people will always resist.

Our basic argument is powerful and simple: there is enough community feeling and support to make a district possible, and enough opposition to make it necessary. That should be our mantra. It sums up what we've achieved in the community and why we need the law.

And when they ask for compromise? We'll look them in the eye and say *the district is the compromise*. Its processes promise everyone the best chance of composing intractable differences and moving toward a more or less agreed upon outcome.

So we will lay a simple choice before the Council. They can turn us down and wait for future community conflicts to come to them. Or they can vote to pass those problems off to a forum—a HPC—better suited to finding **accommodation** among contesting interests where they touch upon historic resources.

I know what I'd do if I were in their place—don't you? Face it: if you can't get them with this tactic, they're not going to be got.

But hold on. Good news! We won.

OUR SECRET OF SUCCESS

Thrilling, wasn't it, our political baptism by fire, even if it was unnerving at the start? What didn't beat us made us wiser, tougher.

Some preservationists may judge our victory as flawed. They will say we should have shown more zeal for advocacy to put preservation on a less political footing. They may criticize us for abandoning our principles to find a way to win.

Well, if it was a simpler thing we did, it wasn't easy. We confined ourselves to getting what we could by manipulating the forces that constrained us. We schemed to win a vote to change the law by drawing other interests to our side. We inspired, negotiated, and hedged our bets to get agreement. I don't remember giving up our principles, do you?

Elsewhere, others who have aimed first at changing hearts and minds for heritage, and only then the law, have failed. The hard-nosed fight we fought was by result more moral. And not just for preservation. By aiming low, we got more. By speaking to our neighbors' interests and linking them with ours, we warmed them to a vital sense that we're all in this together as we head into the future.

Look at what we accomplished with our two-track strategy: we won the district vote at City Hall; at home we built community.

NOTE

1. You can find the rest in my book *The Politics of Historic Districts: A Primer for Grassroots Preservation* (Lanham, MD: AltaMira Press, 2007).

FOUR

A Community Compact for Rooted Growth

History is the myth we live, and in our living, constantly remake.

—Robert Penn Warren

In the postcampaign euphoria of victory you'll find yourself wanting to visit other historic districts. Each will have an ordinance, and most will have a set of guidelines mapping out the scope of its regulatory intent. Some will care for a bare minimum, reflecting political realities and Bill Clinton's maxim, "If you can't get a dollar and you can get a dime, take a dime every time." Others will be quarter, half-dollar, six-bit, or even pricier districts.

If you're like me, all the streets and buildings will begin to blur together in your memory. But what will stand out is the pride in which every district is held, and the sense of purpose and accomplishment of those who show you around.

A COMMUNITY ETHOS

The lesson you will learn is that community, not preservation, defines the prevailing ethos of historic districts. And let's be honest. What's preserved in most of our districts isn't nearly as impressive as the rare quality of civic life we see in the very fact of citizens caring for a legacy, no matter how common.

"It's not much but it's ours," a small-town preservationist told me. What do you do at a time like that? Nod and smile, or politely look perplexed? I say that I do preservation politics, and comments like his speak volumes about the civic good health of a district.

OUR GREAT ACCOMPLISHMENT

Here's how I see it. Historic structures serve as touchstones of civic memory. They remind us that what we do lives on after us.

A community that cares for its past by districting is a community dedicated to being responsible for its future. A historic district says to us: *Here is a place to invest a life, raise a family, grow a business, retire in security.*

"They can offer me a million dollars and I'm never moving," says Paula Soest in the historic district of Orange, California. "You're getting more than a house here; you're getting a neighborhood."[1]

Getting to this point is a remarkable achievement. As Chief Justice of the Indiana Supreme Court Randall Shepard says, "hopes [are] lifted, communities revived" in historic districts.

A HISTORIC MISNOMER

Historic districts are misnamed if "historic" simply signifies the past. In Mesa, Arizona, preservation officer Tony Felice has spoken about how difficult it is to designate historic districts "because of the myths about historic preservation that prevail. Historic preservation is not putting something in a jar of formaldehyde," he says. "It's integrating [properties] into the future."[2]

No district that I know has folks just wanting old buildings standing around. They expect some benefit from their investments in preservation. But what? As so often in our modern world, Aristotle points our way. In his *Politics* he wrote, "Again, men in general desire the good, and not merely what their fathers had."

The greater good our neighbors want from districting is **rooted growth**.

ROOTED GROWTH

If the term is new, the concept isn't. It's what we argued for in our campaign with preservation-plus. Our talk was filled with attractive ways of building on our past.

Now that we've won, "rooted growth" does a better job than "preservation" of describing our HPC's concern for continuity in change. It more accurately portrays how our neighbors feel about the district, consciously or not. Go and ask them what the purpose of the district is. At first some will say to save the past, because it is expected. Then bring up rooted growth. They will eagerly concur, for it is how they think about the district when they think about their futures.

- Todd Kincannon in Simpsonville, South Carolina, supported creating a district "to preserve the character of [the] downtown, increase property values, boost revitalization efforts and unlock the door to an abundance of state and federal grants already earmarked for such projects."[3]
- Brenda Gunter of San Angelo, Texas, said of her 2011 Jefferson Civic Leader of the Year award in Washington, D.C.: "My story and my award [are] attached to a city as a whole and the importance of a historic district to the city and to the future of our town. . . . I felt very strongly that San Angelo had some wonderful history that we needed to build on."[4]
- Mike Buhler and Anthea Hartig have put their view succinctly: "In San Francisco, preservation protections have allowed the city to flourish without sacrificing its soul."[5]

Rooted growth also better represents the way that others who serve on a HPC think if their main interests aren't in preservation, but in real estate, business, tourism, or economic development. It provides a common set of values and interests that can bridge the gap between them and preservationists.

SUSTAINABILITY

Why choose "rooted growth" and not "sustainability"? Because every historic district embraces rooted growth, but not every sustainable community merits district designation. Rooted growth is more specifically preservationist. Unless you're in the *cognoscenti*—in the know as far as lingo—it's difficult to tell where *heritage* and *change* figure into sustainability. I prefer transparent English. When I use "rooted growth" in presentations, regular folks are quick to grasp my meaning.

"Sustainability" has other drawbacks. For some, it brings to mind the heavy baggage of limited expectations that weigh down environmentalism. Compared to "sustainability," "rooted growth" is optimistic about change and has distinct political advantages.

SEIZING AN ADVANTAGE

"Growth" is the high ground in the public-relations contest between preservationists and developers. Why on earth would we want to cede it to our adversaries from the outset?

As San Franciscan Tim Redford has pointed out, "change and growth" are "key words that anyone who has followed local politics knows are the mantra of developers who want to get rid of historic landmarks."[6] By putting rooted growth at the center of our message, we can steal their rhetorical thunder and get other decision makers, from property and business owners to elected officials, to think about us differently.

We are already used to taking pains to say that preservation is good for stronger local economies. "Rooted growth" helps to underscore it.

One more point: "rooted growth" is a term for all seasons. It imparts energy to preservation even in historic districts that are already secure and prosperous.

PRESERVATION WITHIN CHANGE

So what is rooted growth? It represents the key difference between (a) those who think of district designation as the triumph of preservation *over* change, and (b) those of us who see it as a victory for preservation *within* change.

Rooted growth embraces the creative complexity of our communities. But it also agrees with novelist Ellen Glasgow's observation: "All change is not growth, as all movement is not forward."

- "Rooted" speaks to our neighbors' interests in security against incompatible change.
- "Growth" points to their interests in improving—not just sustaining—their situations.

Growth is qualitative. It covers new construction yet also stabilization, rehabilitation, restoration, and adaptive reuse of historic resources. It includes the strengthening of community, our quality of life, and prosperity.

One more thing: rooted growth is not regressive. It cannot countenance demolition by neglect. It insists on proper, timely maintenance. Because all things deteriorate in nature, including good communities, keeping them in decent repair is a form of forward movement.

ROOTED VERSUS MANAGED

"Rooted growth" has another advantage. It crowds out foolish talk of "managed," "directed," "planned," or "regulated" growth. Those notions make us sound like we know better than our neighbors where it is they should be going.

We don't. Isn't it obvious that preservation works best where homes are enjoyable, businesses are profitable, and communities are livable? But you and I don't get to decide what enjoyable, profitable, and livable are. Homeowners, business owners, and other district beneficiaries do.

They will be the ones proposing change. What's more, we know that they'll be changing, too. Folks come and go. And everyone in time will find their interests changing also. We will have to adjust our expectations to do justice to them all *and* to preservation.

Former Council member Ann MacQuoid in Park City, Utah, spoke sense in her effort to keep their ordinance intact. "If you don't like the HDC," she said of the District Commission, "then revise the guidelines. Let the citizens of this community be involved in city government."[7]

Don't mistake flexibility for capitulation. We're talking about responding to changing interests pragmatically, not giving in to them. We can still stand firm *for* preservation even as we don't stand preemptively *against* other interests.

LIKE A TREE

Think about a tree. Oh, I know it's a hackneyed image. I wish I had a dime for every time I've seen a subdivision sign that boasts a tree. Our district's telling difference is that those signs don't picture roots.

We expect trees to grow and change, with loss and gain. We even look forward to new sprouts and shoots while cherishing moss-backed bark.

That's the way it is with districts, too. When new growth comes, we want to see it connected up to sturdy branch and gnarled old limb and broad, strong trunk and roots that run deep, so it appears grown up and out of and richly smelling of *our* soil, not someone else's, somewhere else.

That's what change within a district is, if it's rightly done. To that we have agreed and pledged ourselves as a community. If not to this, then to nothing.

A PORTRAIT OF A COMPACT

Our tree is just a metaphor. To explain what it means to us, we need a myth. Not a falsehood, but the other kind of *myth*: a justifying, sanctifying, self-explanatory, decision-guiding legend, abstracted from our origins, that acts as a reminder of who we are vis-à-vis the public.

The myth I have in mind is this: our district is a living **community compact**—in other words, if you prefer, a partnership agreement—for rooted growth, within which other owner interests as well as preservation are securely embedded and entwined.

The alternative? In Fullerton, California, preservationist David Zenger lamented the four-foot holes that had been punched for ventilation in the walls of a historic Spanish Colonial high-school auditorium. "All of this stuff happens over and over again in an environment where preservation is not important."[8]

This calls for a new environment, one in which preservation as a distinct set of interests is mainstreamed and assisted by the concept of a community-wide commitment to interlocking values, to a broad panoply of interests, and to mutual expectations.

This is what we have, in fact, in historic districts, even if we fail to emphasize it. And, no, you won't find the compact spelled out in your ordinance, though it may be hinted at in the *whereas*es and *wherefore*s of its preamble. But otherwise its absence is no evidence against it.

As Pablo Picasso told Gertrude Stein, "You paint what you know is there, not what you see." It's like the difference between a portrait and a photograph: one reveals the essence that the other cannot see beneath the surface details.

The surface details of our district are the institutions of the HPC: its law, its guidelines, and its procedures. But underneath and giving life to them is our community achievement, which the notion of the compact perfectly enshrines.

This community compact is *the* great victory of the citizen activists who won the district vote. If our district process breaks, it will be this compact that has broken.

So isn't this a legacy worthy of sustaining? If you agree, then you're already thinking like a **districtist**.

NOTES

1. Michelle Gringeri-Brown, "A Grassroots Effort Pays Off," *American Bungalow*, December 28, 2003, at www.americanbungalow magazine.com.

2. Lisa Selin Davis, "Historic Preservation: Finding Room for History in the Desert; Can Tempe Afford—or Afford Not To—Keep Its Oldest House?" *The Next American City*, no. 4, February, 2004.

3. April M. Silvaggio, "Debate Heats Up over Simpsonville District," *Greenville (SC) News*, August 12, 2004, at www.greenville online.com.

4. Trish Choate, "San Angelo Award Winner Represents City in D.C.," *San Angelo (TX) Standard-Times*, June 21, 2011, at www .gosanangelo.com.

5. Mike Buhler and Anthea Hartig, "Better Living through Historic Preservation," September 15, 2010, at www.sfgate.com.

6. Tim Redmond, "Historic Preservation Fight at the Board," *San Francisco Bay Guardian*, January 25, 2011, at www.sfbg.com.

7. Christopher Smart, "Historic District Panel Debated in Park City," *Salt Lake Tribune*, March 14, 2003.

8. Willson Crummer, "Fullerton: City's Landmark Panel Criticized," *Los Angeles Times*, January 13, 1993, at articles.latimes.com.

FIVE

Thinking Like a Districtist

The reward of one duty is the power to fulfill another.

—George Eliot

"What's a districtist?" you ask. Think about it. The core political fact we've learned so far may be represented as follows:

$$P > HD > P$$

Preservation (P) is about more than historic districts (HD), and historic districts are about more than historic preservation (P).

HPCs are agencies of preservation. Not all preservationists rank the workings of our districts high among their priorities—and yet some do.

On the other hand, there are many folks who care less about preservation than about what historic districts can do for them in securing and advancing other interests. These interests range from personal investments to quality of life to economic prosperity and community development.

Individually or in partnership arrangements, all share a common interest in how change takes place in their communities. This gives them a vested interest in their HPC, though few will commit their efforts to their HPC's success.

So what are we to call those among us whose work is tailored to our district processes?

Preservationist just doesn't seem to fit. It's too big here, too tight there. What about "district activist"? Is a city planner an activist? Not if he or she wants to keep the job. Activist carries too high a sense of partisanship.

So I've coined the simpler term *districtist.** It's hard to say, I know, but you'll get used to it. Go ahead and try it on. It suits you. I think you'll like the way you look.

THE DISTINCTIVE DIFFERENCE

As districtists we are all, perforce, preservationists. Still, this doesn't tell us much.

I've known many self-styled preservationists. Shakespeare asked, "What's in a name?" Evidently many things, if the name is "preservationist." Some are your garden-variety "it looks nice so it's all right" types, but serious preservationists take the Secretary of the Interior's Standards for Rehabilitation seriously.

Districtists work hard at getting preservation right. Yet we have a second, equally compelling focus.

---

*Preservationists are used to inventing words. *Preservationist* itself was not recognized by *Webster's New Collegiate Dictionary* fifty years ago.

- As preservationists, we think in terms of preserving the historic resources that characterize our community.
- As districtists, we *also* think in terms of sustaining the political resources that empower our district.

I'd feel a whole lot better about the future if all preservationists shared our district focus. Still, few would take our name and give up "preservationist."

"I don't want to lose my name because that's how I know myself," Moon Unit Zappa says. "There's a legacy here."

Yes, Moon, but we have *two*.

TWO LEGACIES, TWO TRUSTS

As we head into the work of administering the district, we are acutely aware that we bear two legacies:

1. The architectural, cultural, and historic legacy bequeathed to us by previous generations
2. The political victory that we won for district designation

And so with our two legacies come two trusts:

1. A stewardship trust for preserving historic resources
2. A public trust for tending to the community compact that underpins our district

We have to tend to both. With sustained political support, we may accomplish much. Without it, nothing much we do will last.

A MATTER OF INTEGRITY

The way we think about sustaining political support is exactly the same way we think about preserving our district's heritage. The basic concept informing both is **integrity**, not in the sense of honesty but in the sense of a *basic soundness and completeness.*

In preservation circles, we are used to talking about maintaining the integrity of historic resources. We apply the term to individual properties and to their combination across the district's landscape. If an owner removes character-defining architectural details, a building loses its integrity. Then, as entire structures disappear, the district as a whole loses its integrity.

That's how we talk as *preservationists.*

As *districtists*, we also strive to maintain the integrity of community support for the district and the work of our HPC. We can talk about this support in terms of individuals, person by person, as well as in terms of various combinations of people across the whole political landscape of intersecting interests. In losing the confidence of individuals or groups, our district suffers a loss of its political integrity.

When we attend to both concerns—preservation and our community compact—our combined approach has its own integrity by being complete in its two essential parts.

INTEGRAL PRESERVATION

We see this double-barreled approach wherever districts are working well. There is both attentiveness to sheltering historic resources *and* a decent respect for the good opinion of our neighbors and elected officials.

We just haven't had a name for it. So how about **integral preservation** to denote the combination of our twin concerns for the integrity of heritage resources *and* the integrity of our political support?

TWO WAYS OF THINKING

We also see this integrated way of thinking by its absence in our work.

Consider the HPC commissioner who said in a hearing that her job was preservation and it was none of her concern whether the applicant's commercial business—the issue was signage—succeeded or failed. Then there was the state historic preservation officer who was incensed that folks might think differently. "I defy anyone to show me," he said, banging the table, "where it says in state or local law that we're responsible for economic outcomes."[1]

He might be right on law. Even so, don't we have an interest? Shouldn't we be good for business, and business good for us?

That's what your average neighbors think, and so did we in our campaign. It's basic common sense. To them, the individuals making those statements above lack—well, what?—in a word, *integrity* as public servants.

Integrity comes with thinking two ways simultaneously when taking a position, say, on a controversial COA application. You have to ask yourself the following questions:

1. How will what I do comport with preservation law and guidelines as established in our district?
2. How will what I say or do affect the public standing of the district and our HPC?

These are often tense occasions. The answers that we get can be very hard to square. If you've sat on a HPC, you know what I'm talking about. If not, then let's return to Madison, Wisconsin, and do a little role-playing.

POLITICAL TENSION

Imagine you are on Madison's Landmarks Commission and considering the plans to revive the historic 1947 Edgewater Hotel at the price of a new tower block exceeding height limitations, among other issues. The neighboring community has folks supporting both sides. The Common Council is waiting, watching. This is big-time decision making, and you are about to vote. The room is packed, the press is there. All eyes are turned on you.

Do you feel the pounding in your chest? That's the beating heart of politics, quickened by the living spark that plays along a line between two poles, one bidding you to "do what's right," the other one advising you to "be careful" of the political fallout. To act at all takes nerve.

TENSION AS INTEGRITY

Our concept of integral preservation puts this tension at its core. But it isn't a tug-of-war between preservation and politics, where one side wins and the other loses. The best way to think of the interplay is like yin and yang in Chinese philosophy. They are not opposing forces akin to good and bad. Instead, they are contrary and complementary tendencies, interconnected and mutually dependent. The tension between the two acts as a bond between them, holding them together.

And so within our pairing of politics and preservation, as Buckminster Fuller said of architecture, "Tension is the great integrity." As long as we keep this tension at the center of our thinking, the structure of integral preservation holds. Without it, the political architecture of our district starts to fall apart.

NOTE

1. In these two examples and elsewhere, I will occasionally quote individuals or summarize their positions without attribution, understanding that nothing useful could be gained by calling public attention to them by name.

SIX
_____

Delivering Good Government

What government is best? That which teaches us to
govern ourselves.

—Goethe

The greatest long-term threat to historic resources isn't the sap-
ping of our will to save them. It is our neighbors' loss of trust in
districting.

This is almost never a one-time event, which once occur-
ring may be corrected. It is instead a soft sediment of senti-
ment piling up against us because of what we do or our omis-
sions.

It is ever a paradox: it is easier to govern good people than it
is to govern well ourselves.

CHAPTER SIX

THE HIGHEST MORALITY

Administering the district well is a form of moral endeavor. So was winning district designation. Why? Because, as we asserted, winning would advance the public good.

Now that we've won, we must tend to practicalities. Here we might take our cue from Robert Kaplan's reference to "the belief that making the system work constituted the highest morality" in ancient regimes from Mesopotamia to China.[1]

That sounds like mighty good advice for us today, when all manner of public institutions are held in low repute. As I write, the *Washington Post* reports that a *Post*-ABC poll finds that a mere 26 percent of Americans are optimistic about the future when "thinking about our system of government and how well it works."[2]

So pause and take a bow. Remember our campaign? We beat those numbers soundly. We convinced a solid majority that we would make the district work to their advantage. Their faith in us inspired their trust in government.

And now all around us, what? Twenty-six percent.

That's beneath us. Whatever others may be doing wrong, we can't. Not if we're to keep our populations with us for the long haul.

JUDGED BY POLITICS

As servants of the people, we are not the final arbiters of what works and what does not. Our property-owning constituents are, though others have important interests.

Back in our campaign, it was easier to read their verdicts. Now their "vote" is a good deal softer. It's not much more than general feelings that accumulate in a culture of compliance, or of resistance and complaint.

Not only must we make the system work, it must be *seen* and *felt* as working in the HPC, then over backyard fences, at dinner parties, on Facebook walls and Twitter—anywhere that people meet. The repeal of the twenty-year-old Monterey historic district in Virginia was supported by a majority of residents who were, as described by a celebrant, "fed up with what they called 'arbitrary decisions,' 'ego clashes,' 'arrogance,' and 'bureaucratic restrictions.'"[3] Politics created our district and politics will judge it. Accurate or not, perception is everything in politics.

OVERREACHING AND UNDERPERFORMING

Of course, we can't expect folks to take to HPC procedures with affection. Complying with the district is, as Samuel Johnson said of reading Milton's *Paradise Lost*, "a duty rather than a pleasure."

Happily for us, many of our neighbors are favorably inclined our way, at least in the beginning of our administration. We saw to this in our campaign. After designation, they want us to succeed. As for the rest, as we told the City Council, those who stand apart may need to feel the HPC's authority compelling compliance.

Because we're new to administration, this potent combination of favor and power can be intoxicating. We may be tempted to overreach for preservation. As Thucydides said of the Athenians in the aftermath of battle, "their extraordinary success made them confuse their strength with their hopes."

How can we avoid this fate? Where do we begin? Because the exercise of power is the essence of government, we need to grasp its inherent limits.

AUTHORITY AND POWER

We can't make folks like our decisions no matter our *authority*, which is not the same as *power*. The authority we have only lets us try to influence their behavior.

So what is power? It isn't a commodity. We can't actually hold power, store it up, add to it or deplete it outside of action. Power is just a relational concept between people. We don't even know if we have power until we try to use it.

We might have a lot of *paper power* on the HPC. Some commission chairs are ordinance thumpers. Margaret Thatcher spoke to them. "Being powerful," she said, "is like being a lady. If you have to tell people you are, you aren't."

We can cite our authority all we want. But to lay claim to power, it must be recognized by others and move them as we wish. No matter our authority, we will be seen as powerless if we can't achieve our ends. Power is like the wind: it is known by its effects.

While overreaching alienates property owners, underperforming carves away at our standing with those who share our preservation goals. Robert B. Tierney, who has headed New York City's Landmarks Commission (LPC), responded to Tom Wolfe's criticism by affirming that the LPC has "a superb record and a lot has been done." But more than a score of preservation groups and associated parties took the LPC to court over claims of unresponsiveness and nonaccountability. Judge Marilyn Shafer's ruling in 2008 was critical of the LPC's performance, including failure to make timely decisions. Allowing applications "to languish is to defeat the very purpose of the LPC," she said.[4]

POWER AND GOOD GOVERNMENT

Do you see what this means for good government? Governing well is, if nothing else, *the fruitful exercise of power.*

So we won't find good government lodged somewhere in the institution of the HPC itself, in the excellence of its goals and law, or the brilliance of its guidelines. As commissioners and staff, we may even achieve a process that we assure ourselves is transparent, consistent, predictable, and efficient. Yet if it isn't also *effective* in getting good results, it won't be supported by the public or, if it comes to it, by our City Council.

NURTURING COMPLIANCE

Our condition is unique. We are acutely aware of the fragility of historic resources. When the law is broken, it may be repaired by penalties. When an original window is broken and discarded, it's gone forever.

You know what this means: Saturday's do-it-yourselfer has more power than Monday's enforcement officer. What we need more than law itself is the sort of action on the part of the HPC that fosters and sustains a public culture of compliance.

So we ought to ask ourselves, why do folks obey the law?

Of course there is the fear of punishment. But we need folks' cooperation, not mere obedience, or else our district rests upon compulsion. Politically, that's deadly.

What else, then, keeps folks respectful of the law?

Is it true, as historian Arthur Herman says, that "the better ordinary people understand the law, the better the law"?[5] Possibly, unless familiarity breeds contempt. But let's not kid ourselves. No one really reads our ordinance—have you?—or cares as much as we do about mastering our guidelines. Most folks know the law only as they *experience* it.

You and I: *we are the law.* Or so they come to know it by going through our process. The better their experience is *of us*, the stronger is our district law and their respect for it.

For example, my neighbor Matt Herban is restoring a house in Worthington, Ohio. I asked him what their guidelines were like. He responded by telling me "what a pleasure" it was going through the process. *That's* what I'm talking about.

On the other hand, a couple who moved to Evansville, Indiana, to open a B&B sued the local HPC in Vandenburgh Superior Court three years after purchasing their property, having gone round and round on approvals. "To go back to the Commission would be futile," the owner said. "They called me an outsider and were extremely contentious. We would rather have a [courtroom] jury of our peers."[6]

Then there's Barry Guillotte in New Iberia, Louisiana. He spoke up in a meeting to oppose making their preservation advisory board a regulatory board. As a business owner who had renovated six buildings, he described his experience with his first property before the Downtown Historic District Commission. Had the HDC not just been advisory, "I would have been too scared," he said, to proceed with the other five.[7]

Say what you will, such fear is real and poignant. That's why, in the final analysis, the burden of creating a culture of ready compliance falls on us.

FACILITATING ACCOMMODATION

To keep property owners with us, we need to reach accommodations on COA applications. Some may call it compromise, but it isn't.

Do you remember how in *The Godfather*, Marlon Brando looked offended, raised his eyebrows at the other dons around the table, and asked in his raspy voice when had he ever refused accommodation? Would Vito Corleone *compromise*? Fuhgeddaboutit.

Accommodation is adjustment and adaptation, a mutual fitting in. With us, it finds a place for preservation in other interests, while finding room for them in preservation. As we pursue accommodation, we're working toward a common better end than we could have without it.

The *Augusta Chronicle* in Georgia has carried a letter complaining that the Aiken HPC "over the years has failed to use its expertise to help Aiken citizens solve their problems [with] commonsense solutions." For example, "If the preservation of historic homes is a goal of the commissioners, then they should be concerned that homeowners are provided with solutions that are cost effective." The writer believed that the HPC "would rather see a historic home totally lost to the city rather than allow" such solutions. Unless the HPC reconsidered its "goals," he concluded, "they will lose all credibility with the community."[8]

If our district is the compromise, as we told our City Council when we won their vote, then **facilitating** accommodation is how we make it work. We jeopardize our authority when we can't get agreed-upon results.

A dispute pitting church officials against preservationists in Peoria, Illinois, led an observer to write about "the philosophical divide between the two groups." Former City Council member Jim Bateman, then president of the Central Illinois Landmarks Foundation, said, "There is no easy middle ground." Attorney Brian Meginnes concluded, "I think it's inherently a political question that needs to be addressed by the Peoria City Council."[9]

Meginnes may be right, *unless* the HPC has the political insight and steel to structure an accommodation within the discretionary framework of its authority.

DISCRETIONARY DECISION MAKING

Our local ordinance and guidelines are the banks through which decision making flows. The width of our discretion depends upon their terms and the exactness of their language.

Within those banks, HPCs develop interpretive practices. Some keep closer to the side of strict interpretation of their law and guidelines, while others show more latitude. The choice is politically important. The greater the latitude, the easier is the process of accommodation.

No matter where HPCs come down, some folks may take exception, depending on their interests. They typically charge HPCs with "subjective" or "arbitrary" decision making. Such complaints miss the mark. Interpretive decision making is *always* subjective, as it requires judgment. But its legal framework guards against arbitrariness. As long as HPCs keep within the banks of their discretionary authority and follow proper procedure, their decisions are responsible according to their terms of reference.[10]

STREAMING ACCOMMODATION

As a process, accommodation *streams* along, application by application, much as a stream of water finds its way across a challenging landscape. So I like to use "streaming accommodation" to reflect our community-wide agreement to use the HPC for a continuing conversation—*punctuated by authoritative decisions*—in which our common interest in keeping historic resources in play engages the widest array of competing interests for the sake of rooted growth.

It means that year by year, scores or hundreds of projects— perhaps even a thousand or more, depending on our district's size—will be vetted through our HPC procedures. Each outcome will then become a partial installment on our common future.

GATEKEEPING HISTORIC RESOURCES

Throughout this process, we stand at the gate, insisting that all preservation-related projects pass through us and meet minimum requirements for approval. In this sense, **gatekeeping** and accommodation are both key HPC *functions*.

But gatekeeping is also an *attitude* toward historic resources that may jeopardize support. Those who are *dispositional gatekeepers* believe we keep heritage resources safe when we remain skeptical of accommodation and keep a wary hand upon the latch.

For some, their mental gate stays shut. One fellow at a preservation luncheon told my table, "My grandchildren ought to be able to experience the historic district exactly as I did when I was their age." Most gatekeepers aren't so silly. Their image of the past isn't a nostalgic slice of time. They base their work on the documented record of what existed at the time of district designation.

Still, every one of them is haunted by a sense of loss. Vetting change becomes for them a zero-sum affair. Every project involving change, major or minor, may be calculated as subtracting from our fixed supply of historic resources and their supporting context.

Even new additions to our physical surroundings may be seen as subtractions in this math. Some gatekeepers like to see them fit in as unremarkably as possible. This attitude toward design may foster mediocrity and a paint-by-the-numbers approach to guidelines.

Guidelines themselves are rarely satisfactory. There is a tendency to treat "shoulds" as "shalls" and "mays" as "musts" instead of treating these statements as discretionary guides. Gatekeepers may fall back on the Secretary of the Interior's Standards to press for a stricter-than-locally-prescribed preservationist approach. Or they may revise their "district rules," as former property owner George Meyer in Tampa said, making them "tighter and tighter" and eventually "unreasonable." After restoring a house in the Hyde Park district, he moved out.[11]

The gatekeeping impulse is also reinforced by playing up to our "preservation base," to those who share our views. It never seems to occur to gatekeepers that this narrowed notion of our political trust—those to whom we are accountable—is politically untenable. Instead, they tend to denigrate and objectify others and their interests. One commissioner said her job was "to preserve the special character of our town," adding: "Not all of our applicants demonstrate this concern."[12]

But should they have to? Isn't it enough that folks go through the COA process and comply? She would probably agree, and yet her tutelary attitude is telling. By calling them *"our* applicants," she has turned them into our supplicants. She and her interests are firmly fixed in place at the center of her attention. And what about those owners' other interests, which they hold by right? We can almost see her shrug as if to say, "Who cares?"

POLITICAL FALLOUT

In San Francisco, Supervisor Scott Wiener has taken steps "to rein in . . . heavy-handed preservationists before they stamp out important development," according to a weekly blog that sums up his view as follows: "In its effort to preserve the past, the Historic Preservation Commission might just be hindering the city from having any kind of real future—one with affordable housing, good transit, and healthy redevelopment."[13]

Wiener takes a dim view of the local ordinance that mandates professional preservation-related qualifications for six of the seven HPC seats. "If we have a commission made up exclusively of advocates for historic preservation—only advocates—that is a problem." The problem, he says, is that the HPC is "unbalanced."

This is a common complaint about HPC bias. Wiener's call for balance suggests that some less preservation-minded folks should also occupy seats on the HPC. But packing the commission, as some municipalities do, is no guarantee of balance, but only of different points of view. Developers, realtors, and builders—no less than, say, architectural historians—can be inflexible and narrow-minded, too, while putting adverse pressure on preservation.

Still, this is no defense of the status quo. The lesson Wiener offers is that gatekeeping is politically unsound.

As my friend Greg Stiverson says, anyone can open and close a gate. He has seen firsthand how a narrow gate closes down community support. As past president of the Historic Annapolis Foundation, he says it "takes more to figure out how to make things work together, without a sense of crossed arms and hunched shoulders like some burly gnome." The problem, he says, is welcoming folks into the process and valuing their interests.

RESTRAINT

Of course, no matter how we perform, the law will still be needed. But you know what common wisdom says: "The government that governs least governs best." Some use it as an antiregulation slogan. But what it really means is this: *The government that governs best is the one that governs with the least compulsion to the best effect.*

So we want to comport ourselves in such a way that our district operates as though based on voluntary compliance. The fact that it's de jure, enforceable by law, we'll save for when we need it. Success in getting good results will give us power when we need it for enforcement, and our restrained exercise of authority will appear to most as just.

EFFECTIVE SERVICE

Our interests lie in guarding against debilitating change while facilitating project applications. It won't be easy. But then we're districtists. We're used to thinking two ways simultaneously.

We're what you call multitaskers. We keep one hand on the gate, even as we greet all comers with the other hand outstretched, with a "how can we help?" frame of mind.

This means that at every step, from picking up application forms to the final hearing, commissioners and staff think in terms of service. Everyone involved should be intent on helping applicants navigate the process to reach accommodation.

The even-tempered, dispassionate commissioner or staff member will let the situation indicate the shape of his or her response to a COA proposal:

1. To act as *gatekeeper* to confront unruly interests
2. To act as *facilitator* to reconcile competing interests

Yet compared with the strategic clarity we had in winning district designation, the way we encounter change can be especially unsettling as we're about to see.

NOTES

1. Robert D. Kaplan, *Warrior Politics: Why Leadership Demands a Pagan Ethos* (New York: Vintage Books, 2002), 139.

2. *Washington Post*, March 20, 2010.

3. L. M. Schwartz, "Precedent-Setting Victory for Property Rights: Local Historic District Abolished," September 8, 2004, at www.prfamerica.org.

4. Historic Districts Council, HDC in NYC, November 26, 2008, at www.hdc.org/blog.

5. Arthur Herman, *How the Scots Invented the Modern World* (New York: Three Rivers Press, 2001), 265.

6. Kristen Tucker and Sandra Hoy, "Price of Preservation," *Evansville Living*, March–April, 2002, at www.evansvilleliving.com.

7. Angel Haney, "Most Oppose Commission Change," *Daily Iberian*, August 31, 2011.

8. Editorial Staff, "Aiken Preservation Group Too Arbitrary," *Augusta Chronicle*, July 3, 2011.

9. John Sharp, "Historic Preservation, Churches Struggling to Find Compromise," *JournalStar*, October 11, 2010, at www.pjstar.com/news/tricounty.

10. See chapter 14 for a consideration of legally defensible and politically defendable decision making.

11. Cindy Rupert, "Historic House Divided," *City Times*, February 22, 2002, at www.sptimes.com.

12. Name withheld, e-mail on file.

13. Erin Sherbert, "Supervisor Scott Wiener Says Historic Preservation Is Overbearing," January 25, 2011, at blogs.sfweekly.com.

SEVEN

The Temptation of Administrative Legalism

If that's the eye of the law, the law is a bachelor.

—Charles Dickens, *Oliver Twist*

How quickly we pass from leading our community to sitting on the HPC reviewing applications for COAs. This startling shift from action to reaction alters how we think of change.

It's mainly out of owners' interests—not our big-picture campaign vision—that the future of the district is being shaped, often as it seems by random chance, by who wants what, and when, and where.

So here we are fresh from making history, now enmeshed in a project-driven process in which the future comes at us piecemeal, application by often-numbing application for windows, doors, and rooftop changes. These get shuffled in with plans for rehabilitations, restorations, adaptations, new additions, and in-kind repairs, as well as public projects and large-scale new construction.

The problem for us now is what author Gregg Easterbrook, in *The Progress Paradox*, calls the "tyranny of the small picture." A Cleveland preservationist worries about approving a teardown for a freeway: "It's a 'bigger picture' than just one building that really matters."[1] His website title is "Preservation Sans Politics," but he's talking politics.

The political impact of our work is easily overlooked when we focus on a single project. "Frankly I was stunned by the level of useless nit-picking that went on," a critic told the Jackson, California, City Council about a HPC hearing on a hotel restoration. He, too, said that commissioners had "lost sight of the big picture."[2]

We talked confidently in our campaign about using the HPC to advance the greater good. And now we get surprised. "We're standing on sand," Gary Prolaska told a Wisconsin workshop as he described the plight of his Plattville HPC. "Things are happening and we don't hear about them until the eleventh hour and then we have to deal with it." Little wonder, then, that each new application may strike us as our one-shot chance to save a historic resource as life goes speeding by.

THE DILEMMA OF POLITICS

Our problem isn't new. The dilemma of politics has always been that of *having to act without there being any certainty that what we do ought to be done.*

Shakespeare understood the problem in *Macbeth*, when Banquo told the witches, "If you can look into the seeds of time, and say which grain will grow and which will not, speak then to me." Indeed, who can say why *this* results and *something different* doesn't?

We cross sabers with the likes of designation opponent Alan Krigman, but his concerns are ours. He writes that designating the Spruce Hill historic district in Philadelphia "may have a raft of unintended consequence [including] destroying the rich diversity of the area . . . and property abandonment."[3] Perhaps we'd like to say we won't let this happen, but good intentions are not enough to see us through. So what are we to do?

The answer: practice prudence, which since ancient times has been *the* outstanding virtue of political leadership. Prudence helps us cope with doubt and gives us courage. It is the disposition first, before we act, to weigh the likely consequences of all our varied options.

Abraham Lincoln, too, knew the essence of what Mark Lilla terms the "openness and unpredictability of human action."[4] He was at first reflective and then deliberate in action. If the end bore his judgment out, he believed his opponents would amount to nothing. But if the end brought his cause to grief, then ten angels swearing he was right would make no difference.

Our issues aren't as big as Lincoln's. Yet when we contemplate what course to take on difficult decisions, we're standing in his shoes. If you're like me, the prospect is daunting. We'd give anything for just a bit of certainty.

So what happens? We may fall into the trap of what I call **administrative legalism**. That's when we end up seeking dependable answers in the details of our laws and guidelines.

THE TEMPTATION

The seductiveness of administrative legalism is helped along by the way that HPCs work procedurally on a *separability-priority* thesis. We require applicants to split off the design aspects of their projects and submit them for review prior to getting building permits and beginning work. It's a functional arrangement. There just doesn't seem to be a better way of doing design review.

But then administrative legalists take the thesis a long step further. They let themselves conclude they *should* separate historic resources from all other interests and secure them first.

A tantalizing notion, isn't it? It's part of a false sense—a sense of vindication—that the way our district works confirms that our heritage is something special that needs shielding on its own.

What's more, we tell ourselves, our neighbors and elected officials must have known it too, deep down. After all, they approved the system. What we did in playing up to other interests was *clever*, really nothing more. Now we're through with that: our opponents are defeated, the district is established, and all we have to do is administer the law.

OUR SELF-DELUSION

I'm not suggesting for a moment that we aren't sworn to uphold our laws and follow guidelines. But the NAPC's *Code of Ethics* advises us to "seek compromises or search for alternatives where necessary to achieve overall preservation goals *and* provide substantial justice for citizens."[5]

As anyone can see, dotting *i*'s and crossing *t*'s adds up to only part of *justice*. What other parts are there? How about the old bugbear of *cost*? In the current deep recession, it would be callow to suggest that "cost" is nothing other than a code word for antipreservation feeling. In Strasburg, Virginia, where the Town Council suspended its preservation ordinance while reconsidering guidelines, resident Carla Wallen testified that "people in this economy cannot afford to restore their historic houses as much as the town may want."[6]

And yet some communities try to craft their guidelines to anticipate every conceivable eventuality. A few have weighty handbooks. I'm reminded of Gerald Kaufman's description of a ponderous Labour Party platform as "the longest suicide note in history."

A passion for the law is commendable, but our district needs our judgment more. We delude ourselves by thinking that reviewing applications by the letter of our law and guidelines is all there is to duty. But it sure is tempting, given who we are.

Most of us who serve on HPCs are new to public decision making. Secretly we know—unless we're arrogant—what Edgar Watson Howe meant when he said, "The average man's judgment is so poor, he runs a risk every time he uses it." We'd all prefer to duck the vagaries of politics, the opaqueness of the greater good, and the elusiveness of justice.

It's so much easier to separate preservation from all else, equate it with the law, and then simply tell ourselves: *stick to the law!* If we do that, follow our procedures, and things work out— then great! If not—well, we'll just go home, put our feet up, say we did our best, and let the Devil take the rest.

POLITICAL DEMOLITION BY NEGLECT

Administrative legalism is what's left after we subtract our hard-won political experience from district operations. It captures how we think and act *when we behave as though we won the district by advocating preservation's merits* rather than through politics and the roping in of other interests.

This reshaped storyline has great emotional appeal. But like all seductive notions, it subverts our real-world interests and turns us into bureaucrats.

Who else but a bureaucrat could write this confidential e-mail? Barraged by applications for questionable improvements and subsequent complaints, a preservation planner wrote: "They're a bunch of spoiled yuppies. There's a law, and they're just going to have to get used to it."[7]

This is quintessential administrative legalism. There is no evident interest in what these property owners want for themselves or how they feel about preservation. All the writer cares about is that they toe the line.

The result? Such insensitivity can't help but lead to political demolition by neglect.

Those who think this way see the law as closed. The way they see it, the law has already decided where we're going from the get-go. It embodies the well-preserved community as potential.

To see it as they do, imagine the law as being pregnant with preservation. If we can deliver on the law, we can deliver preservation. The more intent we are on preservation, the stricter are we about the law. And the stricter we are about the law, the less are we inclined to think about the greater good as involving other interests. What's more, compliance with the law can take place without understanding or acceptance of its purposes.

The brief against this attitude is that it is, in a word, *Procrustean*. According to the legend, Procrustes lived along a road outside ancient Athens where he offered overnight lodging to weary passersby. Those too tall to fit his bed he chopped to size, and those too small he stretched.

IMPOVERISHED EDUCATION

When we treat law this way we also impoverish district education. After all, we think, the law's the law. We don't really need to win folks to it, just instruct them in it. Simple promulgation of our districting arrangements—printing them up, getting them out, putting them on the Internet—takes the place of engaging our neighbors about what interests them.

We see it at our hearings, too. "Have you read the guidelines?" asked a commissioner. "Yes, but . . ." began the applicant, as he pressed a point of interest. The commissioner interrupted testily, "I'm not here to argue with you."

Holy cow! That's *it?* Not even an explanation, much less accommodation? That's government behaving badly. It makes district law, as Dickens said, a bachelor.

Well, perhaps we aren't the suitors we once were. We vowed at designation to be faithful to our neighbors. Now we've got a midlife district crisis brewing.

NOTES

1. CraigB, "More Local History to Be Lost for Freeways?" Preservation sans Politics, May 8, 2006, at www.preservationsanspolitics .blogspot.com.

2. Scott Thomas Anderson, "Public Rallies for National, Jackson Leaders Bypass Planning Commission," *Ledger Dispatch*, June 28, 2011, at www.ledger-dispatch.com.

3. Alan Krigman, letter,*University City Review*, January 2002, at ucreview.com.

4. *New York Review of Books*, July 28, 2007, 29.

5. National Alliance of Preservation Commissions, *Code of Ethics*, at napc.uga.edu/programs/napc/publications.htm.

6. Preston Knight, "After Outcry, Strasburg Puts Historic District Rules on Hold," *Northern Virginia Daily*, May 11, 2011, at www.nvdaily.com.

7. Name withheld, e-mail on file.

EIGHT

The Crisis of Second-Generation Districts

I used to have power, but old age is creeping up on me.

—Chief Dan George, *The Outlaw Josey Wales*

Sooner or later, our historic district enters its **second generation**. Our law remains in place. The HPC retains its statutory authority.

But the time comes when we pass a demographic halfway point, when a majority of owners have now bought into the district without witnessing its birth. Just about every time a property has traded hands, someone has left who figured into getting us where we are. With the exception of a few who take an active interest in the district, the new owners

- Have little understanding of its philosophy and purposes;
- Aren't up on its institutions, law and procedures;

- Don't know its origins, unique local characteristics, defining ethos, or their own social obligations and opportunities as owners in the district and member of our community.

Without our noticing it, our political base in the community has changed out from under us.

TAKERS IN TRANSITION

If that doesn't make you sit up straight, it should. Remember how we divided up our neighborhood in our campaign among Makers, Breakers, and Takers? We won or lost those Takers one by one, and those who came our way made all the difference.

Though neither hot nor cold for districting, they were acculturated to it after designation. Now, by their proportion of the population, they make up most of those who've left. Most of those who have been coming in—by the same calculation—are politically like them. We can't suppose that they will be any less ambivalent about districting than were their predecessors when we first encountered them.

Do you recall how we missed the issue then, when we started our campaign? We *thought* "preservation" and *said* "historic district." Our neighbors *heard* "historic district" and *thought* "government regulation." *Preservation* didn't bother them half as much as *districting*.

Now it is reversed. Incomers *think* "Old Town spaces" and *talk* about the "historic district." We *hear* them say "historic district" and *assume* they include our HPC, our law, and our guidelines.

What we missed before we miss again: they may be favorably disposed toward preservation, but districting is a different matter. Many have only the vaguest notion of what's awaiting them in the COA process. Mostly they just have gauzy feelings for older places or want to profit from them. The district draws them in, but they're passively incurious about its operations.

Our political task remains the same as in the days of our campaign. We have to win these folks over to districting one by one, for as long as our district lasts.

ENCOUNTERING THE DISTRICT

Many newcomers don't even know who we are. As in a recent online posting, they talk about the "historical society" instead of the HPC as a government commission.[1] This confusion is compounded when a high-profile preservation organization grabs all the local headlines or fronts for the HPC on education.

Even if owners see governmental involvement—say, on a letterhead reminder of their obligations—they may take it as merely supportive, a kind of imprimatur. Most folks haven't a clue about how municipalities work. They might be more or less aware that a zoning board has teeth. But a HPC speaking to design or "taste"—come on, *really?*

So they'll also call the HPC a "committee," like an advisory group applying guidelines that aren't exactly rules. As for COAs, newcomers hear complaints that "those preservationists"—not HPC *commissioners*, per se, but "style policemen"[2]—are making owners jump through hoops.

It gets worse. Even if they understand the HPC's official status, they convince themselves there must be a way *around* the process. This may be especially true of commercial investors who have been courted by the City and so expect special treatment.

And when we think it can't get worse, it does. District arrangements get treated like a traffic light without a cop. If property owners can slip projects by without approvals—projects which don't, as they see it, really injure anyone—then "no harm, no foul," they tell themselves.

And worse. Not everyone respects the law by circumventing it. Some don't even think about the law. And so the first time many newcomers become aware of the district is when we cite them for a violation.

EROSION OF HISTORIC RESOURCES

On the evidence, many folks who benefit the most from our arrangements—simply by owning properties—are rather casual about their responsibilities. Mistakes are made with disquieting frequency. Historic fabric is lost. Inappropriate alterations proliferate.

I don't think they actually set out to rob our community of heritage resources or pick their own pockets of value in the process. Commission Chair Melissa Greene in Eureka Springs, Arkansas, says she detects "no malice" but, as reported, "an honest mistake" on the part of owners who replaced a stone wall without approval.[3]

Some folks just can't help themselves. They'll procrastinate till time runs out. Then they'll do things on the sly. Others do unapproved work, keep their fingers crossed they won't get caught, and, when they are, apply for after-the-fact approvals when the damage has been done.

Then, too, owners may go through the formality of our HPC procedures, get a COA, and later violate its terms. Synthetic porch columns may show up where only wooden ones had been approved. A case might be made for their substitution. But that's a call the HPC should make.

Fortunately these dodges rarely destroy large-scale historic resources. They are more on the order of a replaced window or a clumsy repair. Yet even if these depredations don't add up to a "death by a thousand cuts," their effect is scarring. They damage both our heritage and political support.

CAUGHT BETWEEN SUCCESS AND FAILURE

The hard truth is that HPCs get ground down between their successes and their failures in enforcing district regulations.

Consider our successes first. Most districts begin in crisis. Then, as we avoid new crises, folks relax. "Where's the fire?" they ask, and want us to ease up.

Planning Commissioner Dave Brauwer in Narberth, Pennsylvania, has warned against a "death by a thousand building permits," the "slow erosion" of support that Chair Jim Cornwell says is "almost imperceptible on a day-to-day basis."[4]

Similarly, early San Francisco activists are credited with "saving fantastic structures with true historic and aesthetic value." But "the process is so intrusive now," a critic says, that "such unnecessary interference would be amusing if not for the costs."[5]

Then there are our failures. Folks expect fair enforcement. When we don't deliver, they grow cynical and disconnected. They start asking "What's the use?"

Case in point: Andrew Jones, a property owner in Manhattan's Greenwich Village, reflects on his difficult time with the

Landmarks Commission over custom replacement windows. He is bitter that a neighboring building received an after-the-fact approval for aluminum windows after taking out originals dating to the 1830s. "The message that Landmarks sends is that if you try to comply, you get hassled, but if you do something illegal, you can get away with it."[6]

MISREPRESENTATIONS

How folks form their opinions adds to our distress. Many go a long time without setting foot near the HPC. But here and there a neighbor does. It's their stories that get passed around.

In Maryland, preservation planner Emily Paulus says, "There's a misconception that the HPC denies a lot of applications. . . . The one or two horror stories that have kind of permeated, often times from years ago and other commissions, don't die."[7]

After a while, everybody knows some tale or two of woe. But most don't have an inkling about what we do time and again to reach accommodation.

In Janesville, Wisconsin, the *Gazette* reported in 2010 that a recent count showed that out of 120 COA applications, only 4 had been denied, with just one appealed.[8] And yet a pervasive sense of difficulty led a member of the Planning Commission to suggest a procedure for mediating between applicants and the HPC.

The last year I chaired our HPC, the president of the local residents association invited me to speak. "A show of hands," I asked. "How many of you think we turn down 30 percent of applications?" A few hands went up. "Twenty percent?" Quite a lot. "Ten percent?" Almost everyone else. When I told them that over the previous three years it had been less than 2 percent, I could see the doubts.

And something else, less definable. Sensing it, I said, "Of course, maybe you think we should have turned some of those down." I said it smiling, but I knew I'd struck a nerve.

SERIAL MISUNDERSTANDINGS

Not everyone wants the HPC to find a way to get to "yes" on every project. They're not commissioners-in-waiting who have studied up on our ordinance, guidelines, and procedures or stay abreast of how we reach decisions. What they think we do, or ought to do, is out of sync with us.

An example from Annapolis: Our guidelines direct the HPC to protect public views of the waterways that frame the district. Some residents overlooking a waterfront project testified that it would block cherished backyard views. When we pointed out that those were unprotected *private* views, they were *not happy*. A year or so later we had a similar situation on a smaller scale. Same testimony, same explanation, same result.

NIMBYism—"Not in my backyard!"—got them to the HPC. But **OIMBYism** describes their serial disconnect.

OIMBYISM

The well-administered HPC may be consistent and predictable. The participation of our neighbors isn't. Unless a specific project affects them personally, we don't see them or hear from them directly, on the record. They engage our district process *only when a project is in their backyard.* Even then their participation tends to be undependable.

In Cheshire, Connecticut, Chair Jeanne Chesanow of the Historic District Commission said she "was very disappointed in the turnout" for a hearing on changes to the review process. Only three of thirty-seven notified homeowners attended the meeting. If more didn't come to the next meeting, she said they'd just assume "they're satisfied with the changes."[9]

Good luck. More likely, owners in such situations have mentally checked out. Not only do we lose their active engagement, but those who make regulatory changes will find it easier to tighten up oversight, if they're so inclined. The last time we fine-tuned our guidelines in Annapolis, a few expressed relief that only five noncomplaining folks came to our workshop.

THE SUBTLE PRICE OF INDIFFERENCE

Where we think as gatekeepers or administrative legalists, our own inattentiveness to our neighbors' preferences gets repaid in kind by indifference to our guidelines. Instead of shaping compliant projects, they become afterthoughts. Why should we expect applicants to work preservation into their plans when we ourselves have grown less creative about the role of preservation in their lives?

Folks can't opt out of our district, but their interest and investment in quality projects may take a walk. Then we find ourselves mired in monthly meetings held by jaded commissioners and staff, processing pedestrian applications that add little to our districts and less to our future prospects.

OIMBYism is our aging district's biggest problem. During our campaign we inspired in folks a broader, optimistic interest. The arc of their involvement peaked at or in the period following designation, then simply waned.

Wherever HPCs have been around awhile, OIMBYism gives an impression of historic districts running down like unwound clocks.

NOTES

1. Nicky Boyette, "HDC Hits a Wall," September 14, 2011, at www.lovelycitizen.com.

2. Cheryl Allison, "Narberth Considers Form Zoning to Preserve Town," September 15, 2011, at www.mainlinemedianews.com. Narberth is considering zoning-law changes, possibly including designating a historic district and creating a historical-architectural review board.

3. Boyette, "HDC Hits a Wall."

4. Allison, "Narberth Considers Form Zoning to Preserve Town."

5. Sherrie Matza, letter, *New York Times*, June 20, 2011, at www.nytimes.com.

6. Alexandra Bandon, "The Landmarks Commission Approves Most Requests, but Some Homeowners Complain about Arbitrary Decisions," *New York Times*, December 5, 2004, at www.nytimes.com.

7. Erica L. Green, "Historic Preservation Commission Criticism Not Supported by Numbers," January 22, 2009, at www.gazette.net.

8. Marcia Nelesen, "Commission to Consider Historic Overlay Change," *(MD) Gazette*, April 17, 2010.

9. Luther Turmelle, "Just Three Turn Out in Cheshire to Hear Proposed Historic District Rule Changes," *New Haven Register*, February 8, 2011, at www.nhregister.com.

NINE

Rooters and Rotters: A New Political Who's Who

May God defend me from my friends; I can defend myself from my enemies.

—Voltaire

It's time I posed a question. If you could turn back the clock to D-Day Plus One—the day after district designation—what would you do differently?

So what do you say? Shall we go to the City Council and ask them to repeal our district? Maybe put a sunset clause in our ordinance? You know: by such and such a date we have to demonstrate community support for reconfirmation. How much support? Let's make it 10 percent more than at designation. That should prove we've kept our promises.

It should also stir up our neighbors and shake them out of OIMBYism. At the very least, they'll consider what they'd lose by failing to re-win the Council's vote.

Of course, they might yet decide to let our time run out.

RESETTING FOR
SECOND-GENERATION POLITICS

Even if we don't close down and restart the district, nothing stops us from resetting *ourselves*. By this I mean shutting down to think afresh as though we were campaigning.

Let's set a scene. Say you've called a public meeting billed as "District Sunset Cruise or New Beginning?" The local hall is packed. A hush falls as you get up on your feet and scan your neighbors' faces.

What are you looking for? Comfort from surefire preservationists? Be careful. Some of them won't stand by our preservation record, which can never match ideals or satisfy everyone. Yet others with other interests will.

What you really want to know is who stands behind the district by their actions, and who doesn't. You're going to need an analytic tool to tell the difference. May I suggest something sharp and simple, despite its sounding fancy?

RAISON DU SYSTÈME

What do I mean by *raison du système*? Well, you know raison d'état, right? It's a phrase left over from Voltaire's age, when French was the language of diplomacy. We still use it in translation as "reasons of state." It holds that the interests vital to the survival of a state take precedence over other interests. Without the state, forget the rest.

Similarly, I'd like you to think of *raison du système*—"reasons of the system"—as summing up our overriding interest in the durability of our district institutions. It means that we should stand for this with deep conviction: *the greater the support for the HPC and its authority, the better are the prospects for ensuring rooted growth and preservation in the process.*

Our perspective is as follows:

- If we approve a controversial project—the HPC must stand.
- If we lose an important property—the HPC must stand.
- In good times and in bad—the HPC must stand.
- As our district ages—our HPC must thrive.

We have already seen trouble brewing with OIMBYism and the effects of changing attitudes and demographics both on and off our HPC. Those are general tendencies.

Now we want to look specifically to see who across the district's political spectrum might be labeled district **Rooters**—whose actions sustain our roots in the community—as opposed to the **Rotters**, who are a source of rot.

AN OVERVIEW

Neither group is homogeneous. I find it helpful to divide Rooters into three rough subgroups:

- **Actors**, who are engaged in actively sustaining the district process
- **Backers**, who support but do not regularly engage the process
- **OIMBY Slackers**, who support yet carelessly engage the process

Similarly, Rotters are of three sorts:

- **Shirkers**, who by their casual violations evade the district process
- **Shredders**, who by their egregious behaviors pose more subversive threats
- **Should-Know-Betters: Preservation Radicals**, who support preservation while endangering the district's standing.

ROOTERS

A commitment to the integrity of heritage resources goes only so far. Rooters support the district, while the degree and quality of their engagement affect the integrity of its political underpinnings.

Actors

Actors are the ones who do the district's work. If they didn't, it wouldn't get done. They form the backbone of our community's investment in historic districting, working out in front or behind the scenes. They are our political base, and we are part of them. They stick with us through thick and thin.

Not all Actors have the time or resources to take a leading role. Many would like to be able to do more. Others do more than their share.

Actors are members of our community or have strong ties to it. They stand foursquare for districting, testify at hearings, and may take a turn on the HPC. They also tend to cycle through leadership positions in other related organizations.

Outside the HPC we see Actors as

- The *practical advocate*, speaking out for the HPC;
- The *public servant*, caring for district operations;
- The *elected official*, protecting the HPC's role in public decision making;
- The *newspaper reporter or editor*, accurately portraying district issues;
- The *president* and *board members* of a heritage group, supporting the district process.

The society of Actors peaks at designation and thins with time as the intensity of the political moment passes, interests change, and activities compartmentalize. As Actors deactivate their involvement, they slip into the ranks of Backers.

Backers

Backers are more passive. Originally, they helped win the campaign for district designation. Today, they and others like them support the district but are less actively engaged.

Nonpreservationists may be civic-minded individuals or associations who supported designation but now keep a lower political profile while they promote the welfare of the district through, for example, a business association. The local heritage society might also prefer to stay away from district issues that could cost them membership or cause fund-raising problems.

Individual preservationists may also prefer to turn their efforts to less political pursuits, perhaps relating to preservation as

- *Single-interest preservationists*, who specialize in aspects of preservation;

- *History preservationists*, who are in it for connections with the past;
- *Cultural preservationists*, who value the refinement of preservation;
- *Social preservationists*, who enjoy the society of volunteers;
- *Philanthropic preservationists*, who underwrite the work of preservation.

They care about the district in different degrees, and all do useful things. Their various interests and endeavors reflect the healthy diversity of the preservation movement. Good thing, too, as none of us can do everything that needs doing. They free Actors up to focus on district operations, and the stronger preservation is because of their activities, the stronger is public appreciation for the role of preservation in the life of the community.

The same goes for nonpreservationists who contribute to community development. The more prosperous the district is, for example, the better is the case for preservation as contributing to the greater good.

Above all else, let's remember the *good citizen*, whose law-abiding compliance with HPC procedures is the lifeblood of the district. Good citizens are Backers by result even if not by interest or intent.

OIMBY Slackers

Common in larger, aging districts, OIMBY Slackers maintain only loose ties with our district process. They support the district when and how it suits them. The greater their disengagement, the more likely are they to have views formed outside the serious work of the HPC in defining rooted growth by COAs, in accordance with our ordinance and guidelines.

We may find among them

- *Self-referential preservationists*, who hold their views to be as valid as the HPC's;
- *Beautification preservationists*, who equate preservation with loveliness;
- *Improvement preservationists*, who think in terms of market value;
- *Good-taste preservationists*, who equate preservation with style;
- *Appearance preservationists*: "If I drive down the street and it looks okay," one said, "that's the standard."

They, as well as non-preservation OIMBYs with interests in the district, tend to be all over the board on regulation and enforcement. Some press for a strict approach, while others favor relaxed oversight. Some newcomers even import understandings of how we ought to work from other districts.

They have a right to their opinions, and we appreciate their interest. But they lend strength to the impression that there is no strong community consensus behind district policies and practices.

This shortcoming isn't theirs alone. It suggests a retreat of political leadership on the part of us Actors since district designation—*our own slackness*, if you like—and our failure to retain their engaged support.

ROTTERS

Rotters distinguish themselves by the way their attachment to their own interests works against our standing in the community.

Shirkers

Shirkers duck the HPC's approval process. Honestly? Most folks shirk sometime. What wins someone the Shirker label is (a) willful neglect, if not outright intent to skirt the process, plus (b) repetition. Those who fall into this pattern define themselves by their actions as minor-echelon opponents of preservation and historic districting.

Their acts are small and mean. They install a vinyl window, use improper mortar for minor repairs, or fudge on business signage. Such violations are like pebbles dropped into a pond. They don't attract much attention with their little ripples, but they encourage similar behaviors.

Shirkers undercut the district in the following ways:

1. By harming the integrity of historic resources
2. By harming the political integrity of the district process

Most could not care less about preservation. A few are self-avowed preservationists who are careless about their district obligations: though their unapproved projects may be compliant, their behavior toward the process isn't.

Shirking can be like crack cocaine: try it and you're trapped. If you do one illegal project, how can you do the next one right, if it means on-site visits by commissioners, staff, or city inspectors who may detect the first? So not only do wrongful projects get done, even necessary repairs and worthy projects may go underground.

Some owners struggle with the guilt or stop when fined. Others don't, and may in time slide into the ranks of Shredders.

Shredders

"Vulgarity begins at home," said Oscar Wilde. Shredders are historic district vulgarians. Unfortunately, what begins at home often shows up *on* their houses, too—even on their porches.

In the Greensboro, North Carolina, College Hill Historic District, a feud erupted over students who held that sofas and upholstered chairs out front were traditional expressions of property rights. Resident Noel Jones described them as "people who assert that they don't have to do what the rest of us have to do, which is abide by the historic district guidelines."[1]

Shredders are aggressively antisocial. They are openly in our faces all the time. "George Washington could've slept there," a Virginian says about his home. "I don't care. I sleep there now. History is just what it is, the past."[2]

Shredders do more than undercut the district: they swing axes at it. They endanger historic resources and shred the community ethos that distinguishes our district. They raise shirking to the order of a principle of action. Some think of themselves as standing heroically against intrusive government.

Shredders often include those Breakers and their allies who rode out our districting campaign. They remain a major reason for having the district. Among their number, we know them as

- *Radical property-rightists*, who cloak themselves in libertarian doctrine;
- *Egotists*, "my way" individualists, who are focused on their own self-regarding interests;
- *Contrarians*, who will always stand against consensus;
- *Power-trippers*, who are out to prove us weak;

- *Payback plotters*, who are out to get even for defeats;
- *Too-big-to-fail investors*, who dare us to turn them down.

They don't care a whit for preservation. They might say it gets in the way of progress, or carries too high a price—or any one of a litany of other reasons. When you open each one up, it's an empty closet, just a place to hang the Shredder's hat.

Shredders flaunt the law. The most egregious sorts are often nonresident owners. Others are spreadsheet-bottom-line barbarians. Seeing no self-interest in the good order of our district they are, in a word, disorderly. They

- Let their properties deteriorate through neglect;
- Bulldoze historic buildings on the slightest legal pretext;
- Strip their buildings of original architectural details;
- Make major inappropriate repairs and alterations.

The worst of them throw junky work at their properties like litter at a trash can. They hire the cheapest contractors, who care nothing for historic fabric. If they can't evade the HPC, they'll aim below our minimums, then afterward cut corners or make unauthorized design changes or material substitutions.

Confronted, they may raise the stakes and sue. A few will spend more money on fighting us than it costs to do things right. Even when they're caught and fined and the fine holds up, they may drag their feet and never set things right.

These Shredders are like leeches. They suck value from the district, especially from their neighbors. They are social cankers, and their properties often open sores. As William Powell said in *The Last of Mrs. Cheney*, "Tragic. I blush for them."

Should-Know-Betters: Preservation Radicals

A few folks feel that heritage needs protecting from everyone, including HPC commissioners and staff who disagree with them. They think they are our betters. But in fact, they should know better. They do untold damage to our district.

Shredders make a principle of interest. But these preservationists make *principles* their interest and their guide to action.

We know them as

- *Keepers of the flame,* who see themselves as preservation purists;
- *White-glove preservationists,* who won't dirty up their hands with politics;
- *Vigilante preservationists,* who circumvent the HPC to scare off projects;
- *Prophetic preservationists,* who project an ideal district beyond practicalities;
- *Phoenix preservationists,* who instigate crises to give rise to purer practices;
- *Scorched-earth preservationists,* who advocate enforcement minus justice;
- *Paranoid preservationists,* who see conspiracies against preservation everywhere;
- *Preservation martyrs,* who are proud to be attacked for the sake of preservation.

We see them in many forms, or many forms in one—and yet, if we're lucky, never on the HPC.

If they serve, they do deserve some credit. But they aren't natural consensus seekers, except for their point of view. They use guidelines to attack noncompliant project applications rather than for working for agreement. Majorities may have to do without them, as they are quick to cast dissenting votes.

We have to work as hard on them as we do with Shredders to find practical solutions. They give Shirkers added reasons to skirt the HPC process, Backers extra incentives to shy away from politics, and Actors the added burden of having to defend the HPC on two fronts. They bedevil confidence and comity and flay community support.

We feel no affection for Shredders. These Should-Know-Betters are different. We'd like to like them for the sake of preservation. Instead, we think of them as in the words of William Blake: "Thy friendship oft has made my heart to ache."

NOTES

1. Jim Schlosser, "Neighborhood Feud over Cleanup," *News and Record*, August 29, 1999.

2. Sally Voth, "Vinyl Siding, Windows among Concerns Expressed at Strasburg Joint Meeting," *Northern Virginia Daily*, May 10, 2011, at www.nvdaily.com.

TEN

Our Strategic Line

Float like a butterfly, sting like a bee.

—Muhammad Ali

Now the question is: how should we respond to all these folks?

First, let's be clear: every one of them is equal before the law. As a quasi-judicial body, our HPC is designed to serve all equally according to due process.

Yet *they* relate to us differently, as suits their attitudes and interests. So while we treat them equally, we need a nuanced strategic line in responding to the various ways they engage us.

The great English political philosopher Thomas Hobbes knew when and how to fight. "Be sociable with those who will be sociable," he wrote, "and formidable with those who won't."

Memorize his line. We're going to build on it from here on out.

REVIVING COMMUNITY SUPPORT

We've tried to live up to the expectations of those who supported us for district designation. Still, our record since then isn't all that we intended, for many reasons—some due to us and some to forces that beset us, including demographic changes.

As our district ages, we should pledge ourselves anew to comport ourselves so as to resuscitate their trust, while eliciting good citizenship from newcomers. We want all those we serve to feel they're better off with us than without us, despite our flaws.

That's our goal. But as we encounter resistance, we should be prepared to be *formidable* with anyone who is hostile to the purposes and proper functioning of the HPC. This will impress our law-abiding neighbors who are watching us. With all the rest we will be *sociable*: solicitous, understanding, positive about accommodation, personable, considerate, compassionate, and encouraging as leaders.

As we pursue our strategy we are, as Ralph Waldo Emerson said of Walt Whitman, "half song-thrush, half alligator."

WORKING WITH DISTRICT ROOTERS

Rooters are sociably inclined toward our historic district. We should respond in kind and guard against drift in our relationships. Yet our sociability must retain an edge where behaviors are inconsistent with the interests of the district, which are uppermost in importance.

Working with Actors

A society of civic-minded Actors is more important than good laws in a historic district. But Samuel Johnson knew that "the most fatal disease of friendship is gradual decay, or dislike hourly increased by causes too slender for complaint, and too numerous for removal."

As our district ages, we should strive to keep all Actors in the loop, up-to-date on policies and practices, while tolerating one another's shortcomings. We also need to guard against the tendency to narrow down the circle to committed preservationists. The toughest task is socializing others, to find the right folks to put in the right place to serve the broad spectrum of our community's interests in districting.

Working with Backers

Yet even as we try to draw new Actors from the available pool of Backers, the latter over time tend to subdivide. *Strong Backers* still agree on the importance of sheltering historic resources while respecting the efforts of the HPC to work with other interests. *Weak Backers* may lean one way or the other:

- *Preservationists* may back the district as a heritage shelter without feeling especially obligated to support accommodation.
- *Nonpreservationists* may back the district as an engine of community development without caring as much about sheltering heritage resources.

Still, when Backers speak on current issues, they typically do so from an informed perspective on our ordinance and guidelines, practices, and procedures. Our being sociable with them helps to keep us focused on our common goals. Otherwise, they slip into the third rank of district Rooters.

Working with OIMBY Slackers

These folks weary our sociability. Preservationists who take seriously the Secretary of the Interior's Standards also struggle with them within the larger preservation movement. Districtists may encounter OIMBY Slackers in crises—"hearing today, gone tomorrow"—advising us of our duty or upbraiding us for our faults without much more than a cursory awareness of our policies, practices, and precedents.

Some fall into the trap of administrative legalism. They are most egregious when they try to use the HPC process to settle scores with their neighbors or get at underlying use. They study up on technicalities and demand that we deliver, and they sometimes sue us if we don't.

We want to be sociable, but we end up having to correct them pointedly—if civilly—in meetings when we think we shouldn't have to, when it embarrasses everyone involved. Their distant OIMBY orbit makes it hard to keep them in the loop. Efforts to reach them sociably are usually conducted through traditional outreach education.

DEALING WITH DISTRICT ROTTERS

Those who tax our efforts at delivering good government deserve a formidable response, even as we strive to deal sociably with them. Teddy Roosevelt offered good advice: "Don't hit at all if it is honorably possible to avoid hitting; but never hit soft." Having the sustained support of the community on our side puts oomph behind our punch.

Dealing with Shirkers

Shirkers renege on details of our community compact. But it's a stretch to call them "antisocial." Test it. Take a Shirker aside and say, "Don't you see what you're doing?" "What—*that?*" he'll interrupt, nodding toward his small-scale projects or re-pairs. "Lighten up, it's no big deal," he'll say. "It's just in my backyard."

JIMBYism sums it up.

Yet explaining their behavior is like swimming through mashed potatoes. Maybe Shirkers just can't be bothered, or are tired of going through the process. Perhaps they've had an unsatisfying experience with the HPC. Then there are absentee owners for whom the district is a foreign country.

Some Shirkers buck the process because they didn't have a hand in its creation or don't like those of us who run it. Still others might not be especially law-conscious people in their daily lives, or just dislike property law in particular.

Some are merely cynical, thinking they have to know how to play the system and hire the "right" architect or contractor, even an attorney. Most of these will grudge the fees or other costs involved. A few see the review process as judging *them*, personally, and bristle at the prospect. Some are otherwise good folks who simply fear public forums and are afraid they'll fail themselves.

All of these—and you're welcome to add more—are specula-tive explanations. But not one justifies bad behavior.

We have to be formidable to arrest their serial violations. Yet compared to Shredders, these folks may be open to sociable inducement.

We should underscore the community ethos behind districting. To socialize them into our community compact, we should approach them with the understanding that the world is full of good people who do bad things—including even us upon occasion. We should be firm and neighborly to win them to a culture of compliance.

Dealing with Shredders

Shredders bring out the best of the worst in us. If we apply all our formidable powers to stop district Shredders, we will be viewed as being sociable toward everybody else.

When difficult owners appear before us, we owe it to them, to ourselves, and to the rule of law in our community to give them squeaky-clean due process and every discretionary advantage we would offer anyone. We should be civil even when fining them for violations. "When you have to kill a man," Winston Churchill said, "it costs nothing to be polite."

But those who are formidable with us should know our limits. Will we actually be able to look past their unruliness? "Every normal man must be tempted, at times," H. L. Mencken wrote, "to spit upon his hands, hoist the black flag, and begin slitting throats." Is that us? Well, let them bring it on and see.

Dealing with Preservation Radicals

Dealing with preservation radicals is ticklish. Ronald Reagan admonished the party faithful against speaking ill of other Republicans in public. We don't want to subvert the many good works preservation radicals do beyond the HPC. But I think we can support them while heeding Neil Kinnock's sage admonition to the British Labour Party: "Loyalty is a fine quality, but in excess it fills political graveyards." That's why I prefer Boston Celtics coach Red Auerbach's approach to Reagan's. He could criticize his players and his friends, he'd tell reporters, but they couldn't.

We should try to remonstrate sociably with these preservation colleagues. Many are deeply informed, even professional preservationists. We could benefit from their expertise if they'd show more willingness to pitch in with us to find practical accommodations

What distresses us most is that they hang aloof or claim to engage us as the "loyal opposition." But we've got their number. They may be loyal to preservation, but they are not loyal to public service. They give every indication of caring more for historic fabric than the living texture of people's lives.

A passion for heritage may also prohibit the sort of questioning that is essential to accommodation. "Architecture is one of the great arts," says a preservationist in a state-level fight here in Maryland. "You wouldn't take a painting and rearrange it. Why do it with a building?"[1]

Purists in historic districts adore this sort of "case closed" rhetorical flair. If we question their positions, we'll be told in effect to give up our questioning. Why? Because if we were true preservationists, we wouldn't question them; and, if we're not, we won't respect their answer.

Doctrinal confidence is a kind of arrogance—and worse: it strikes us as intimidation. We shouldn't try to prove our bona fides. We'll respond sociably to find value and cooperation where we can. But when purists touch on politics, we must take them on, on the grounds of ideology, which is hostile to good government.

NOTE

1. *Baltimore Sun*, October 26, 2005.

ELEVEN

Dealing with Preservation Ideologues

If stupidity got us into this mess, then why can't it get us out?

—Will Rogers

Radical property-rightists and preservationists clash over heritage. But when it comes to politics, some of our more doctrinaire colleagues share a common characteristic with their opposites: both act from ideologies.

THE NATURE OF IDEOLOGY

What makes them *ideologues*? As with ideologues of every stripe, they arbitrarily reject some aspect of reality to build up their image of how things ought to be, according to their principles. We see hints of this in their "if only" approaches to government:

- Radical property-rightists say, "*If only* the HPC would get out of my way . . ."
- Radical preservationists say, "*If only* the HPC would do what I say . . ."

Both positions conclude, "*then* my corner of the world would be a better place." What's missing from them both is an acceptance of contending interests, which is the stuff of politics. And so the interiors of their images of our communities are strangely depopulated.

- Radical property-rightists are individualists who live in a small world of their own, a world of one.
- Radical preservationists see historic districts like the recent guest at our inn who got up at dawn to take photographs. "It's so hard," she explained, "to get pictures without people getting in the way."

During our campaign, we avoided doctrinal positions in shaping our pragmatic strategy of preservation-plus. By the same token, we took on and defeated our property-rights opponents.[1] Now we must confront preservation ideologues whose ideas and behaviors subvert the community compact that we won.

TRANSCENDING POLITICS

There seems to be something politically disorienting in whatever gives rise to a hard-core preservation aesthetic—something that fosters "a desire to transcend . . . politics rather than engage in them, with the unsatisfying moral compromises which that entails."[2]

That passage is from Robert Kaplan's writing on an entirely different topic: idealists in international affairs. I cite his line because I'm struck by its resemblance to e-mails from someone who criticized a HPC for "playing politics," that is, for acting from any but the strictest lockbox reading of its preservation mandate. "Preservation has standards," he wrote, "that transcend politics, *n'est-ce pas?*"[3]

I rather like that "*n'est-ce pas*," don't you? It's a French-fried version of "you dolt!" But I'm afraid the rest is overdone.

FILTERED STANDARDS

Strictly speaking, preservation can't have any standards, can it? It's an abstract concept. It's *we* who have standards *for* preservation.

We use the same verbal sleight of hand in the oft-heard phrase, "in the interests of preservation." Really? There are only *our* interests *in* preservation, about which we may disagree among ourselves. That's why we've developed standards, to harmonize our practice.

We may imbue these standards with moral significance, but that's just us. To others with competing interests, they are at best suggestions.

Politics comes into play when we want these other folks to comply with our standards and they demur. Then it is our interests versus theirs, and politics decides the outcome.

Take the Secretary of the Interior's Standards—shall we say our *standard* standards? They were promulgated with political support at the national level. From there they've filtered down. The closer to the ground they get, the more they are particularized, admixed with other interests, and then made concrete through local politics in our historic district ordinances and guidelines.

That's because such general advisory precepts cannot be applied in their abstract formulation. Those who would give them effect must concern themselves with local needs and other conditioning factors, including concerns for justice and the consent of the governed.

In Oak Park, Illinois, the controversial plan to expand the boundaries of the Frank Lloyd Wright Historic District offers two distinctly different sorts of regulations for the four hundred homes to be included. HPC Chair Christina Morris assured residents that the Commission wanted their approval. "We don't want to plow it through," she said. "[This] is something we want to do, not something we have to do."[4]

THE POLITICS OF PLACE

It's obvious then, isn't it? No matter what we think preservation is *ideally*, what preservation is *concretely* happens place to place: it's found within the politics of place, in each historic district.

This is clear to anyone who has gone through a districting campaign. What comes out of each is framed by the following:

- What we want for preservation
- What our neighbors want for themselves
- What we offer them specifically
- What they can support
- What we can agree on
- What the City Council will approve

Every districting proposal goes through this process. It's what makes preservation in Charleston uniquely *Charleston preservation*; in Santa Fe, *Santa Fe preservation*; and, in your town, *Your Town preservation*.

It's why local standards for a snaggletoothed downtown corridor desperate for investment dollars will be different from those for a prosperous midtown mansion neighborhood or a highway-lining farming community. Each has its own unique set of interpretive standards, guidelines, and practices. They can't be held accountable to, nor are they interchangeable with, anybody else's, or any abstract, ideal notions.

Even once they're set, our work is never finished. The NAPC's *Code of Ethics* advises that we should "continually evaluate and update [our] plans, ordinances, standards, guidelines and procedures to ensure they meet the community's current and future needs."[5] Adjusting standards to fit changing needs is the work of politics properly conceived.

People who claim that their take on principles trumps this process engage in a dangerous conceit. That's not the way that districts work, so it can't be good for preservation.

TWO VIRTUES

Preservation ideologues like to claim the courage of their convictions. But as noble as that sounds, they are confusing two types of virtue:

1. A private virtue that underlies a personal commitment to preservation
2. A public virtue that inspires service to the district

As private citizens, they may elevate what they deem to be right for preservation above all else, and pay the price for doing so alone. Those of us who hold the public's trust may not. An ability to discipline personal values to the practical work of sustaining the authority of public institutions is always and everywhere a sign of political maturity.

AUTHORITATIVE PRESERVATION

We need to be coldly assertive about what preservation is when HPCs rule on project applications. By the authority of our ordinance, it is *how we call it.*

Outside of that, there's only—what? Well, no matter who testifies before us, they offer us the same thing: *opinion.*

- The keeper of the white-hot flame? Opinion.
- The professional giving expert testimony? Opinion.
- Our local heritage foundation or statewide preservation office? Opinion.
- A private-sector preservation trust? Opinion.
- Legal beagles telling us the law? That's opinion, too.

Do you know who they are? They're not us. We take their testimony, weigh it, and then decide.

Three umpires, as the story goes, were asked how they called balls and strikes within the rules of baseball:

1. The newest ump allowed, naively, "I call them as they are."
2. The next up in experience smiled and said, "I call them as I see them."

3. The oldest, wisest of them all, replied, "They ain't nothin' till I call 'em."

That's how it is with us. Our call decides balls and strikes on COA applications. That's what gets recorded. Whatever else preservation might have been was only penciled in, erased. This side of the appellate process, our HPC is *the* preservation authority for our historic district, under law.

CORRUPTING POLITICS

To justify their stance, some preservation colleagues may quote Lord Acton's observation that "power tends to corrupt" and its corollary, "absolute power corrupts absolutely."[6] We as public servants know something more important: *absolutes corrupt power* on the HPC.

Bear that in mind when you confront them over issues. Don't go looking for a fight. But if they want one, Hillary Clinton has said it all: "You show people what you're willing to fight for when you fight your friends."

As long as you keep your political wits about you for the sake of public service, you'll never get caught punching above your weight.

NOTES

1. See my chapter on "Skirmishing with Radical Property Rightists" in *The Politics of Historic Districts: A Primer for Grassroots Preservation* (Lanham, MD: AltaMira Press, 2007).

2. Robert D. Kaplan, *Warrior Politics: Why Leadership Demands a Pagan Ethos* (New York: Vintage Books, 2002), 98.

3. Name withheld, e-mail on file.

4. Jim Jaworski, "Residents Skeptical of New Historic District Boundaries," March 22, 2011, at www.triblocal.com.

5. National Alliance of Preservation Commissions, *Code of Ethics*, at napc.uga.edu/programs/napc/publications.htm.

6. John Dalberg-Acton, letter to Mandell Creighton, April 5, 1887.

TWELVE

Political Personalities: Who Leads?

The measure of a man is what he does with power.

—Plato

We have parsed who's who in our district and put ourselves in the forefront. Now we have to be as objective with ourselves as we were with others. Leadership reveals itself in many forms, not all of which are equal or equal to our tasks.

How we respond to change is telling. Change in our aging district puts stress on historic resources and district institutions. It also stresses us. Some of us are energized. Others batten down the hatches and just soldier on. Some embrace integral preservation, while others are attuned to administrative legalism. Some facilitate accommodation, and others throw up roadblocks.

All can find good reasons for their choices. The traits that bring us to lean one way or the other are *intellect and temperament*. The combination of the two defines our *political personality*.

So what do you say? Shall we turn our sights on ourselves?

FOUR POLITICAL-PERSONALITY TYPES

Good. Now, then, how do we recognize and put together what we see? We'll do it systematically, by sketching out four basic political-personality types as they relate to Thomas Hobbes.[1] Leaders may be by intellect and temperament

1. Sociable and formidable;
2. Sociable, not formidable;
3. Formidable, not sociable;
4. Neither formidable nor sociable.

This typology can help us better see ourselves, understand our differences, and compensate for each other as we can.

Type 1: Sociable and Formidable

These Actors are self-confident and flexible in their roles. They take pleasure from positions of authority. As sociable optimists, they anticipate change as affirming the vitality of the community even as it brings them problems.

They are assertively positive about the role of government, enthusiastic about working with others, and comfortable with exercising power. Their priority lies in making the district work, and they look for better ways to do it.

They are proactive in conflicts. They seek out the toughest issues, cultivate support, and expect to win. They assume the district is only as strong as the HPC's last success and its next decision.

Yet they are not unnerved by loss. Whether they succeed or fail—and they expect to lose sometimes—they don't take it personally or demonize their critics. They know that politics isn't about them. So they readily adapt to fluid situations and change their minds as conditions warrant.

They are team leaders, power sharers, consensus builders, facilitators. When singled out for credit, they deflect it off on others to empower them to do new things tomorrow. They inspire confidence and loyalty by their example.

Relaxed in their own political skins, they're not laid-back but energetic. Never ones to flinch from exercising power, they prefer jawboning and brokering to relying on the law or their prerogatives. They will put their foot down when things get out of hand and enforce the district vigorously when they have to.

They take their cues from observing what's going on around them rather than from abstract notions about what's right and proper. Being solution oriented, they are ideologically neutral. They think like Deng Xiaoping: "No matter if it is a white cat or a black cat; as long as it can catch mice, it is a good cat." They are pragmatic decision makers.

In HPC meetings they are fast off the mark and quick to get to the heart of things. They use the process to accommodate conflicting interests, which they see in positive-sum terms. They know how to run smooth meetings, and they handle political tension well.

Being both sociable and formidable, they are risk-taking, happy warriors for the district. They leave highly charged sessions energized.

Though they obviously enjoy commission service, they may be rather less attentive to administrative details. Used to thinking politically, they prefer to be where the action is. If they cycle through the HPC, they look for other things to do to make a contribution. They take on public education to draw others into their arc of service and accomplishment.

Privately, they like to think that, with them, the historic district is in capable hands.

Type 2: Sociable, Not Formidable

These Actors are compliant, rather politically passive and easy-going folks with ingratiating attitudes. Their impulses are social rather than political.

They lead from the center, optimistically encouraging others to get along to go along. They want to be a friend to everyone, and have everyone be a friend. They desire all the drama of a Doris Day movie.

This preference for sociability reflects their discomfort with exercising power over neighbors. They enjoy authority for the chance to help, though they also like to be admired for their contributions.

Because politics puts them ill at ease, their priority lies in being well-received as the key to job performance. They substitute likability for political success in sustaining community support. They figure if folks warm to them, they will like the district, too.

They accept the challenges of change, while counting on an outwardly sunny disposition to see them through its challenges. Risk averse, they have a "sure, why not?" kind of optimism.

This makes them reactive problem solvers. They like to be thought of as Mr. or Ms. "Fix-it," typically telling others, "I'm here for you," "Bring me your problems," and "Let me know what I can do." They say it with a smile that often masks an underlying personal uncertainty about their ability to handle conflict. Confronted by a difficult project, they'll say "We'll see what we can do," while meaning, however, that they'll let the district process run its course.

While they look to good outcomes, they prefer to stay above the fray. They favor accommodation to disarm conflict rather than for working through it. They are sympathetic, scene-setting shapers more than doers. With them, as Mark Twain once said, "Action speaks louder than words, but not nearly as often."

In the HPC, they like to get things off on a friendly footing, sit back, see what develops, join the popular side if need be, or pour oil on troubled waters in the role of peacemaker. If they take an active role in deliberations, it is often as the go-to master of technical requirements, detail, and precedent, which they use to press for happy outcomes.

They see themselves as team players more than leaders, preferring to sit in circles and defer to others. Not quite sure of themselves, they readily adapt their views in a changing climate of opinion.

In confrontations, they verge on being genial nonentities, not foxhole sorts of folk. They sense they can't be formidable without jeopardizing their own and the district's reputations for being helpful. They dread saying no.

This opens them up to being manipulated and marginalized when the chips are down. So they aren't eager enforcers. If they have to do it, they'll passively let others lead.

They convey a friendly competence and efficiency, which inspires a kind of trust. They may be able, open-door administrators. As long as things are going well in a stable district, they can do a splendid job, friendly at the helm.

Privately, they like to think they put the right face on the district.

Type 3: Formidable, Not Sociable.

Al Capone would tell Type 2 folks, "You can get much farther with a kind word and a gun than you can with a kind word alone." Type 3 Actors like the gun part best.

Formidable and rarely sociable, they see themselves as hard-duty district sheriffs, shooting down noncompliant projects and enforcing process. They expect little but problems to come from change, and for them everything is zero-sum.

They are anxious about staying ahead of the curve or falling behind. For them, "losing feels worse than winning feels good," as Vin Scully said about baseball. They value wins mostly for what others lose. When they lose, they think of getting even. They like to tote up wins and losses.

Offensively oriented, they head in the direction of gunfire. They watch for emerging problems and then ride out to head them off, brandishing their authority.

They like to exercise power, but don't take much pleasure from it. They come across as highly driven to deliver good government to a less than deserving community, often feeling they give better than they get in recognition.

They seem to have tough hides, but they're thin-skinned underneath. Challenges to heritage and the HPC are taken personally as threats to their authority and what they care about. They sense that the district is only as strong as they are.

They are, as a type, pessimistic about others. As loners who distrust team playing unless they're in control, they are disinclined toward power sharing. Just the opposite: they jealously protect their prerogatives. They'll put on a sociable performance if it will get them what they want.

Yet they tend to be confrontational in HPC meetings. Conflicts over interests and policy quickly become personal, creating situations that end up confirming their negative pre-conceptions.

Often perfectionists themselves, they are drawn to the exactness of the law. They take a rather hard line on guidelines and equate accommodation with compromise and weakness.

This makes them rigidly incapable of adapting to any other point of view. They feel betrayed by colleagues on the HPC who don't support them, and they rarely hesitate to cast dissenting votes when it suits them, often as a point of honor.

As administrators, they're feared more than valued for their my-way-or-the-highway thoroughness and tenacity. In outreach education they are aggressively assertive about the HPC's authority. They think of it as putting the community on notice.

Privately, these embattled Actors believe the district can't survive without them.

Type 4: Neither Formidable nor Sociable

These folks are leaders only in the sense of holding a leadership position. They often find themselves with authority they neither want nor enjoy. Some, not all, serve as commissioners because they've been dragooned or as staff because it is a job.

It's hard to know how they see themselves, but low self-esteem seems to fit. Certainly they tend to be thin-skinned and withdrawn. Like tortoises, they're slow to act and quick to retreat into the protective shells they build around themselves. They don't go the extra mile—or, indeed, the extra step—to make the district work. They might wonder why the tortoise ran at all in Aesop's fable.

Theirs is a fortress mentality. They prefer to work "behind the scenes," as they might call it, where they labor miserably at what they see as thankless tasks for the sake of duty. They mean well, but do only what they have to do in clearly defined tasks that they perform unimaginatively, and sometimes not at all. They are often good folks who, feeling battered and disheartened, have just burned out.

Feeling isolated and underappreciated, they're quick to defend their inaction in terms of their job descriptions or the limits of their authority. "My hands are tied" is a common comment. Rather than increasing their own or sharing power, they are relieved to cede initiative and authority to others.

As HPC commissioners they let others lead, while they may come unprepared and then sit back. They offer applicants neither help nor criticism, except pro forma. They prefer to agree with other commissioners in meetings that end early.

These unsociable and passive pessimists have a stop-the-world-I-want-to-get-off attitude toward change. Insensitive to its opportunities, they react slowly to its threats, while waiting for our HPC procedures to kick in for them. They seem to think that the district, having been wound up at designation, will keep on ticking with or without their contributions.

Uncomfortable with politics, they insist on law and principle, even though their aptitude for self-protection makes them malleable. They cringe at enforcement and fear reprisals. They'll bend or ignore regulations and procedures—on the q.t.—to extricate themselves from trouble. When forced into accommodating change, they'll do it to be rid of problems.

They tend to be both principled in their own minds and inconsistent in practice. If they get caught with their necks out, they'll turn turtle quickly.

Otherwise, they see themselves as functionaries, processing project applications. As in-box, out-box administrators, they believe folks ought to know the rules and shouldn't need a nurse-maid. "The form is self-explanatory" may be a favorite phrase.

They're averse to outreach education. Unless they're tasked to do it, they don't. They dread public forums and are quick to turn defensive under questioning.

If working with others is unavoidable they'll comply, while expecting little out of it and viewing everything as a bother. They know if they do more, more will be expected. They seek refuge in chains of command and run from turf battles. They think like Martin Cruz Smith in *Wolves Eat Dogs*: "Figure out the food chain, and you figure out the world."

Privately, they want to be somewhere else. But we may find them, as sometime Texas politician Hickey Freeman says, "hangin' in there like a hair in a biscuit."

SUMMARY

So what is the response of each political personality type to the challenges of change? Let's sum it up in four brief phrases:

1. Sociable and formidable: Good government.
2. Sociable, not formidable: Good me.
3. Formidable, not sociable: Good offense.
4. Neither formidable nor sociable: Good grief!

Whichever types we are ourselves, most of us have to work with some version of every type in our district operations. What's more, our constituents have to deal with all of us. We need to find a way to work together in decision making.

NOTE

1. I have modeled this typologically on the active/positive matrix developed by James David Barber in *The Presidential Character: Predicting Performance in the White House*, 3rd ed. (Upper Saddle River, NJ: Prentice-Hall, 1985).

THIRTEEN

The Stages of
Declining Historic Districts

Education is a progressive discovery of our own ignorance.

—Will Durant

Our individual political personalities shape the character of our HPCs. We reveal our temperaments in decision making, and our constituents experience us as we treat them.

So how do they find us: sociable or formidable? Would we agree, or are we too close to ourselves to observe objectively? "Many a man's reputation," essayist Elbert Hubbard wrote, "would not know his character if they met on the street."

I once turned the corner and saw a vaguely familiar face studying a building. "I know you, don't I?" he greeted me. I told him I chaired the HPC. "That's right," he said. "You're the rat bastard who approved my roof."

Me? He must have meant someone else! Or did he lump us all together?

A DECLENSION OF HPCS

Let's imagine the kinds of HPCs we'd get if each one were populated or even just dominated by one personality type, from the best to worst. We'll give them pub- or rock-band names for fun. Here goes:

Type 1. Sociable and formidable: The Up & Doing

Type 2. Sociable, not formidable: The Open Arms

Type 3. Formidable, not sociable: The Regulatory Spanking Machine

Type 4. Neither formidable nor sociable: The Muddle On

Now let's this take this one step further. In book 8 of *The Republic*, Plato develops a typology of societies based on the intellects and temperaments of those who define their politics. He ranks them top to bottom. Then he traces how a society declines step-by-step as it descends the list.

You're ahead of me already, aren't you?

A DYNAMIC OF DECLINE

Isn't that the way it is above?

I don't mean it literally, historically. Maybe it does or doesn't work that way, like bumping down a flight of stairs. Still, it can serve us as an allegory of how districts and their HPCs come to split off from the public.

We'll assume that the best HPC is found right after designation. Its members still act from the political lessons they learned from campaigning. The community remains close and supportive at first. From that point on, our district starts to come apart politically as it ages.

So here we go again, aware that if Plato wrote today it would be for cable television, maybe with a soundtrack. Let's make it R&B. Did Plato ever get his groove on? I would like to think so.

Stage 1: The Up & Doing

In the beginning, the HPC is filled by those who most closely follow Thomas Hobbes, who are up and doing for the public, making good decisions, aiding applicants, and enforcing the district process. We hear Marvin Gaye and Tammi Terrell singing "Ain't No Mountain High Enough," which works rather well either sociably or formidably, you know, depending how you hear their pledge not to be deterred. But our type 1 commissioners don't get much positive feedback from their neighbors who have gone back to their daily lives. The press won't cover the good work they do, nor will gossip; both, however, trade in failures or mistakes—or worse: distortions. Those outside the process come to feel there's something wrong going on with the HPC, even if there really isn't. OIMBYism begins its slow retreat from consensus and support. We then catch snatches of Gaye singing "I Heard It through the Grapevine," all alone. Old campaign pros cycle off, and those who take their places want to put a better face on district operations.

Stage 2: The Open Arms

The first HPC is followed by those who try to smooth things over by easing up, overlooking slights, and smiling as they cozy up to owners' interests. They are determined to get along with everyone and have a good reputation. Al Green's version of "What a Wonderful World" sets the scene. But soon the HPC is accused of rubber-stamping COAs. Then these sociable commissioners are taken advantage of one too many times by those who aren't sociable with them. Now the pendulum starts swinging the other way, with strains of the Tams' "What Kind of Fool Do You Think I Am?" rising in the background.

Stage 3: The Regulatory Spanking Machine

Type 2's formidable successors enter to the tune of "Tighten Up," by Archie Bell and the Drells. Sociability takes a powder on all sides. The process shifts from amicable to adversarial. Predictably, the Drells play on in an endless loop.

By now the gap has opened wide between the HPC and its constituents. As we've followed this descent, we've learned more and more about how ignorant we get about leadership as our HPC deteriorates.

Stage 4: The Muddle On

At rock bottom, everyone is dispirited about the HPC and the role of preservation in the community. Isolated from public opinion, crabbed in its operations, the HPC slogs along under uninspired leadership. Now it's all B.B. King singing "The Thrill Is Gone" to fadeout.

In this final stage, because the HPC is neither sociable nor formidable, the historic district is disoriented and disordered. The ranks of Actors thin, Backers lose conviction, and Slackers spin still farther from the HPC. Shirkers damage historic resources with near impunity. Shredders get away with murder. Should-Know-Betters rail on behalf of their philosophies, while those owners who once were model citizens grow cynical.

A culture of complaint prevails. Then, as Plato writes of his last stage before collapse, we find impeachments everywhere. Commissioners and staff are set upon in the press and public forums. The political landscape is dotted with lawsuits and appeals.

Something's got to give, something has to bring order. Those who have the power, ultimately the City Council, start to overturn HPC decisions and tinker with the district, and, when all seems lost, they begin considering wholesale changes or repeal.

THE ANTIDOTE

Can nothing save the day, to protect us from decline?

There are two parts to the antidote, which have to work in tandem. One appeals to administrative legalists. I'll stress it as **defen-*si*-ble decision making**, which tracks along with law.

Now, we districtists like law, too, no doubt about it. That's what we fought for with designation. Yet we also embrace **defen-*da*-ble decision making**, which keeps an eye upon our political support in the community and on our City Council.

So let's turn the page. And as we do we'll hum "What a Difference a *da* Makes," with apologies to Dinah Washington.

FOURTEEN

The Politics of Decision Making: Defensible and Defendable

> To do something right does not mean that doing it is right.
>
> —William Safire

Let's take stock of where we are:

- We have considered how we see our task as we respond to change through gatekeeping and accommodation.
- We have analyzed the seductive weaknesses of administrative legalism compared to the political strengths of integral preservation.
- We have learned to deal with others, sociably and formidably, as they engage the district process.
- We have taken our own measure to see whether we are fit or less than able leaders.

Now we have to ask how we might assure ourselves that what we do next doesn't pull the roof down on us.

MADISON'S CHARGE TO US

James Madison summed up our central problem. "In framing a government," he wrote, "the great difficulty lies in this: you must first enable the government to control the governed; and in the next place oblige it to control itself."

Administrative legalism's singular strength lies in focusing on the rule of law in district operations. But then, all well-run HPCs work very hard at self-regulation within the terms of their authority. We follow procedures, ensure due process, and base our decisions on local law and guidelines.

Our principal attention is to *procedural* due process, which assures applicants that we follow established procedures in a fair and timely manner. Then there's the other safeguard of *substantive* due process, which should ensure that our decisions are neither irrational nor egregious.

These are hallmarks of *defensible* decision making.

DEFENSIBLE DECISION MAKING

How often have you heard it said you should "think outside the box"? Have you ever wondered, *what* box? Let's make our commission room our mental box, to set an image. It is filled with us, our law, our guidelines, and our procedures.

We districtists, acting on behalf of our twin legacies and trusts, think inside the box and out, beyond it, to the *ripple effects* of our decisions on political support for districting, the HPC, and rooted growth.

Administrative legalists avoid chasing after these unpredictable and politically elusive criteria. They say to us, stay in the box and master it professionally. The best that we can do, they believe, hearing after hearing for the aggregate of applicants, is ensure an efficiently administered district according to the law.

We do that, too. All of us, regardless of our attitude toward politics, are *formidable with ourselves*: we turn the law on ourselves and hold ourselves accountable for due process and defensible decisions. That's how we are like COA applicants. The law squeezes them, and the law squeezes us. And while the squeeze itself can't ensure that the juice is sweet, the squeeze is still essential.

PROPER PROCESS

Abstractly, defensible decision making looks more or less like this broad-brush summation:

- Administrative staff or some other authority oversees the submission of the application, making sure that it satisfies requirements.
- A HPC session is convened in accordance with the law, including provisions for public notification.
- The meeting is conducted in a manner that ensures due process.
- The project is presented.
- Testimony is taken.
- Commissioners deliberate.

Picture the scene as though you were making a model educational video. Commissioners come to the meeting prepared. As they arrange the application in front of them, you show footage of prior site visits, quiet study of the project's documentation, and review of the ordinance and guidelines. Then a gavel raps. The meeting is opened. Commissioners listen to testimony, ask pertinent and well-framed questions, look judicious, and nod their heads or frown thoughtfully, all the while consulting the variety of materials in front of them. A decision begins to take shape, and next:

- A motion is put forward citing chapter and verse reasons for the project's compliance or noncompliance with local law and guidelines.
- After further discussion, the motion takes final form and the vote is held.
- Done properly, the HPC's process is efficient and its decision is defensible.

COMMISSION TRAINING

Reality is almost always different:

- After more than a year on his HPC, one commissioner asked, "What are these guidelines you all keep talking about?" It really happened.
- So did this. A commissioner in California announced that a project would never be approved because as a seagull in a former life he had flown over the site and hadn't seen it.

Oh. My. Gosh.

Most failings aren't so spectacular—*to us*. But to applicants, even some minor procedural confusion can seem significant. So, too, will unprepared commissioners who take part in deliberations, or any talk about what we do or don't "like" about a project instead of whether it complies. The list of such mistakes is almost endless, as you must know from your own experience.

Regular training sessions in proper decision making are invaluable any time, anywhere, to guard against such errors. And no matter how many training programs you attend, it's like in sports: repetition develops muscle memory. Repeated training helps to make professionalism second nature.

DEFENSIVENESS IN DECISION MAKING

Defensible decision making has to do with quality control. It's rather as if Madison himself were observing us and holding us to exacting public-service standards.

Yet much of our sub-rosa interest in how we make defensible decisions is *defensive*, too. Let's break it out:

- *Defensible* decision making means doing things properly, above reproach, within the rule of law.
- *Defensive* decision making means taking care to get defensible decisions that deliver what we want for preservation in whichever way we frame our interests.

A common example of defensive intent is the temptation to use our guidelines to redesign projects to please our own aesthetic sense. So the question frequently arises, how does a guideline differ from a rule? I once heard preservationist Pratt Cassity cite the following pop culture reference, and I've used it ever since to good effect in presentations.

Did you see *Ghostbusters*? On report of a disturbance, Bill Murray goes up to Sigourney Weaver's apartment. He knocks, she answers. She has a wildly supernatural look about her. She invites him in. He says he makes it a rule not to become involved with women who are possessed by demons. She plants a big one on his lips. "Actually," he says, "it's more of a guideline."

We are tempted, too, to use guidelines to get us what we want.

Charleston's Eddie Bello understands. I visited him in his busy office back when he helped oversee the City's role in preservation. As we briefly chatted, he said the biggest problem they had was in attracting quality design in new construction. The Board of Architectural Review saw it, too, and members would press applicants for better than they offered. He wasn't unsympathetic. But he felt he had to make a special effort to impress upon the BAR that if an application met minimum requirements it had to be approved.

His care was rare enough that the opposite is not uncommon.

If applicants can be strong-armed or plum worn down, most any outcome can be justified within the latitude of guidelines and the law. And as long as we've ensured due process, our decision is defensible.

QUACKERY

But applicants aren't dumb. They know that "defensible" is not the same as "just."

"This ain't some lowlife dirt bag you're dealing with here," Baltimore mystery writer Tami Hoag writes in *A Thin Dark Line*. "He's an architect, for Christ's sake!"

You can bet an architect knows when he's being pecked to death by a duck. It doesn't matter how the duck does it. A competent and efficient duck, a law-abiding duck, a duck that follows all the rules of duckdom, is still a pecking duck.

DEFENDABLE DECISION MAKING

This makes defensible decision making very much like advocacy at the start of our campaign: absolutely necessary for us to master, but not enough to win the day.

Simply put, legally *defensible* is not the same as politically *defendable*. Close attention to law and administration can guard against missteps. But it can't insulate us from the politics that judge us. Bottom line:

- *Defensible* decision making is about protecting our findings by hewing to the law.
- *Defendable* decision making aims at securing the political standing of our decisions in the district and beyond, including down at City Hall when they're brought up on appeal.

The most important community judgment about us isn't whether our HPC does things efficiently by the law or not. It's whether we are seen as being *strong* or *weak*.

Even state-level agencies face our problem. In Illinois, the state Historic Preservation Agency (IHPA) initially permitted the City of Chicago to replace a historic limestone lake revetment with concrete in Hyde Park. Public outcry led IHPA deputy officer Anne Haaker to say the agency "screwed up." David Bahlman, president of the state's Landmarks Preservation

Council, reportedly observed that the IHPA had "not histori-cally [been a] strong agency."

Efficiency is crucial. But even if we don't mess up, when it comes to a crisis *effectiveness trumps efficiency every time* and sus-tains us for the future. South East Chicago Commission president Valerie Jarrett was taking a wait-and-see position on the IHPA's change of direction. For her it wasn't just a question of preserva-tion but of effective results. "Obviously, the goal here is to balance a variety of different public objectives and goals and interests."[1]

We could ask for no better description of the task of *defendable* decision making on our own HPC. We can get everything legally and administratively right *defensibly* and still get bad results.

PROCESS PROUD

In fact, it seems perversely likely.

A lot of us find the field of preservation law and administration to be compelling. It can dominate our attention and eat up all our time. And then as we apply it, it can make us process proud.

We can get so wrapped up in our administrative practices that we let ourselves get boxed inside our heads—and out of politics, as though it doesn't exist. We are lucky then if we don't find our-selves entangled in enforcement as our neighbors drift away.

NOTE

1. Maurice Lee, "Historic Preservation Agency Focuses on Point," *Hyde Park Herald*, June 5, 2003, at www.savethepoint.org.

FIFTEEN

Enforcement: The Third Rail of Preservation Politics

The first law of law enforcement is, when your shift is over, go home alive.

—Sean Connery, *The Untouchables*

We want an *enforceable*, yet not so much an *enforced* district. Even Thomas Jefferson—no political slouch himself—admitted that "an honest man can feel no pleasure in the exercise of power over his fellow citizens." And *they* don't like it either. This is why districting, not preservation, was our designation problem.

It also makes enforcement like the third rail on a subway line. We need its power to make our district run, but it is deadly if not approached with care.

LEVERAGE

I'll own up. There were times on our HPC when I wanted to use enforcement to mete out punishment to Shredders, pure and simple. A few of them really frosted my socks. But then, as Dwight Eisenhower said: "You don't lead by hitting people over the head—that's assault, not leadership."

Yet a formidable ability to punish violators and enforce our process gives us leverage. We should use our potential to inflict hurt to get Shirkers and Shredders and everyone else to pull up a chair to our table to talk through problems.

A BROKEN CONVERSATION

Looked at this way, the necessity of actually having to enforce the district may be, in columnist David Brooks's useful phrase, "a symbol of the broken conversation" between owners and the HPC. The rule of thumb should be that the greater the need for enforcement, the less attention we've paid proactively to politics.

This makes some commissioners and staff wary of enforcement as an admission of failure. Apart from that, any number of reasons may be adduced for inaction, up to and including care for preservation.

Consider this actual example. Three property owners are within a stone's throw of each other. Each needs roofing work.

- The first, who has an average income, gets approval to replace an asphalt shingle roof, not with in-kind materials, which were permissible, but with an expensive, handcrafted standing-seam metal roof, which would take the property back toward its original condition. The nearly flat pitched roof is barely visible from the ground.

- The second owner, with a more modest income than the first, asks the HPC for permission to replace a much-deteriorated, seriously leaky, structure-damaging, and by expert testimony irreparable original metal roof with an affordable substitute material. Though this roof, too, is hardly visible, the application is denied.
- The third, a wealthy owner with a poor preservation record on numerous properties, avoids the HPC, has a crew hammer down the standing seams of an original metal roof, and clads it in bitumen. The well-pitched roof is visible.

In the third case no enforcement action is brought against the violator, even after he has been advised to stop midaction. Why? The argument is that he owns so many properties in such poor condition, and has been such a serial problem for preservation, that some other, more positive incentives must be found to reset the conversation.

We can sympathize . . . and wait . . . and see what happens. The argument has *preservation* merit.

A BROKEN TRUST

But is our *district* based on the tractability of Shredders? Of course it isn't.

We argued just the opposite in our designation campaign. We spoke to our neighbors' concerns about districting because we couldn't win them with our views on preservation. We connected with them differently. We proceeded partly on the sly understanding that while they weren't themselves eager for regulation, they wanted their neighbors under the thumb. So we undertook to shield their interests from the minority of willful owners who made the district necessary. We assured them that their neighbors, too, would be made to comply with district rules or suffer consequences. As preservation economist Donovan Rypkema has said, "Homeowners have a level of assurance that their neighbors will comply with the rules."[1] Putting preservation first again will look like bait and switch.

We need to enforce our procedures to uphold our end of the district bargain. Not following through on violations constitutes a broken trust, a reneging on our compact.

THE CHUMP FACTOR

And do you know how those folks will feel whose interests are neglected? Like chumps.

Can you blame them? What's more, they will have lost a crucial measure of self-interest in the district and be less inclined themselves toward working for compliance. They're getting there already, as we saw in sketching out the crisis of second-generation districts. There comes a point in their cynicism when "What's the use?" becomes "Get off my back!"

Our neighbors have only so much tolerance and goodwill. On the other hand, Shirkers and Shredders will take advantage of our weakness. As soon as we lose the threat of credible enforcement, they will be on us like rats.

JUDICIOUS ENFORCEMENT

Thomas Hobbes has instructed us to be formidable with those who will not be sociable. Yet there is a caveat. Petty, overzealous enforcement is unattractive to those who would be sociable with us. Enforcement with a human face—and an eye to justice—is appealing.

So we need to take Hobbes's dictum as a guideline, not a rule. In fact, a restrained use of the cudgel can enhance our power to enforce. The opposite can cream us.

Our HPC is a quasi-judicial body, but justice can't be blind. We must always act judiciously in our exercise of authority on behalf of law. It is madness to enforce the law without a decent respect for justice and the feelings of our neighbors.

THE CITY AND ENFORCEMENT

Higher ups in city governments and especially on city councils don't like enforcement. When I chaired our HPC, the mayor told me she never got complaints about nonenforcement, but only the opposite. Well, *we* heard about it regularly on the HPC. The fact is that public officials know their electoral strength lies in new projects with new benefits, not in keeping old things like a district going through the threat of punishment.

One of OIMBYism's costs is that a large segment of the community may expect enforcement but won't press the issue consistently with one voice. A local heritage society may be loath to get involved. Homeowners are reluctant, too. When Strasburg, Virginia, town manager Judson Rex suggested complaining neighbors should report violations, "one woman yelled, 'I'm not a tattletale.'"[2] When the HPC asks for help from the heads of other City departments, we often find to our consternation that authority comes down the line, not up.

There's no easy solution. The best that we can do is conduct ourselves in such a way that those others on whom enforcement depends find it in their interest to work with us. They have to see us as part of their power base, perceive the community as being behind us, and understand that enforcement works for them.

THREADING THE NEEDLE

We have to thread the needle. If we gain a community reputation either for neglecting or for overzealous enforcement, two things will happen:

1. Folks will impeach our judgment and withhold support.
2. Some will appeal our findings, while making *us* the issue.

If appeal is to the courts, we may be shielded by *defensible* decision making. But where appeal is to politically complected bodies, ultimately the City Council, *defendable* decision making can make the difference.

If we've already lost in the court of public opinion—or retain just lukewarm support—then we can't like our chances.

NOTES

1. "Preservation Haul," *Chicago Tribune*, December 28, 2003, at www.chicagotribune.com.
2. Sally Voth, "Vinyl Siding, Windows among Concerns Expressed at Strasburg Joint Meeting," *Northern Virginia Daily*, May 10, 2011, at www.nvdaily.com.

SIXTEEN

The Politics of Appeals

Compromise is the best and cheapest lawyer.

—Robert Louis Stevenson

The appellate process is a meat grinder. Do whatever it takes to stay out of it while getting acceptable results.

A CASE IN POINT

Let's see what happened in Madison, Wisconsin, with the issue we first encountered in our introduction. The Historic Landmarks Commission (HLC) denied the application for rehabilitating and expanding the Edgewater Hotel. Then the Common Council overturned the Commission on appeal.

Adding "insult" to "injury," according to Madison Trust executive director Jason Tish, the Council then "suggested

some debilitating changes to the ordinance and Commission."
"No matter how you interpret" it, he says, "the integrity of the
Landmarks Commission and the Mansion Hill Historic District
took a serious hit."

"There were strong arguments on both sides of the debate,"
he goes on to tell us in his most admirable review.[1] "At its core,
this project pitted job creation and economic development
against the value of preserving the character of a historically significant neighborhood."

But the issue wasn't all that stark. Some features of the
project tracked along with rooted growth. Tish acknowledges
there were "positive aspects to the proposal: the rehabilitation
of the [hotel] and the improvement of the failed public space
of the 1970s addition." He also says that both preservation and
economics "are important pursuits, essential to any healthy city
with a sense of identity, but in a depressed economy, job creation is a tough opponent."

The Commission's decision was agonizing. One commissioner said it was the hardest decision he ever made.

In the end, the vote to protect the integrity of the ordinance
turned out to be, in novelist Dorothy L. Sayers's fine phrase,
"about as protective as a can opener." Tish claimed that it further threatened the integrity of historic resources by laying bare
the ordinance to "major changes by people less qualified to make
them, whose motives would likely be to remove guidelines perceived as obstacles to development."

A QUESTION OF LAW AND ETHICS

What lessons can we learn? Well, none to second-guess the
HLC. As political commentator Jeff Greenfield has said, "Vic-

tory has a thousand fathers; failure a thousand kibitzers." Still, trying to learn from their experience honors their travail.

We may find ourselves in our own districts confronted by a situation in which the law prevents us in good conscience from approving a worthwhile project that's noncompliant. If that's the case, then as the *Code of Ethics* suggests, perhaps it's time to change the law.

But this case also warns us against proving the advisability of revision to our City Council in such a way that inclines them (a) to take the law out of our hands and (b) to take it out on us, our district and our HPC, and the community we serve.

If our law and guidelines still serve our district well, and what's before us is an important one-off issue likely not to be repeated, then we ought to find the strength to approve it. But if we can't find a way to "yes," then we're better off working toward an exception on appeal that leaves our district law and guidelines still intact.

And don't forget our campaign promise to the City Council. That was when we pushed for the district with our politically inspired claim that we could keep such issues off their plate. It was good strategy. We believed, as does Tish, that we are better suited for dealing with these problems than they are. We owe it to our basic trusts to prove it.

THE IRON LAW OF APPEALS

I have an iron law for any HPC staring at a volatile issue: *Let it end with you.* Don't just find for your ordinance and guidelines. Find a way to make them work, or change them. You have a district to defend.

This imperative does not make the dilemma of politics any less disturbing than it actually is. Take the example of another hot hotel issue, in Milwaukee, which followed closely on the Madison affair. Here, after project backers conducted a withering campaign, the HPC gave them "everything they wanted," said James Draeger, the deputy officer for the Wisconsin Historical Society. "They folded like a house of cards," agreed Alderman Robert Bauman, who also sits on the HPC.

The outcome? Mayor Tom Barrett decided, as reported, that it was "time to look at the 30-year-old law and see if it still reflects what the community wants."[2]

The lesson? Work aggressively for mutual accommodation and think politically. Remember, folks are judging you as strong or weak. If you can make the process work to find a way to crack the hardest case without giving in, you will be seen as formidable.

Getting to "yes" has a caveat. If the other side is simply bloody-minded, then let them know you'll take them to the mat and fight them on appeal. It may give them a religious moment and convert them to tractability.

Alderman Bauman said of the HPC: "The only way you could blunt a campaign like that is if everyone stood together." He himself was considering resigning from the HPC. "There's no sense in staying if the commission ceases to perform its core function."

Sometimes, as Vince Lombardi said, you don't lose the game so much as time runs out. Yet every coach knows that if the game had been played with the same determination all along as it was when the clock ran down, then the outcome could have been different. With a solid reputation for pragmatic balance, practical cooperation, and clean due process, you will be in a stronger position if you have to play in overtime on appeal.

DEALING WITH A LOSS

If you lose, so be it. Don't complain.

The best advice comes from Phoenix attorney Rory Hays, who told an NAPC training session that if the decision goes against you, "accept it and move on."

THINKING THE UNTHINKABLE

The time may come when folding is nonetheless the wiser choice. If you find that unthinkable, then keep this analogy in mind. It stunned me when I heard it.

It came from no appeaser, but the author of the hard-nosed doctrine of *containment* that won the Cold War. George F. Kennan was a career diplomat, adviser to presidents, and Pulitzer Prize–winning historian. As the dean of political realism in American foreign policy, he argued that had every country that declared victory at the end of the First World War simply surrendered at the opening shot in August, 1914, every one of them would have been better off, stronger, safer, and more prosperous in the long run.[3]

What he knew is this: some good fights aren't worth the fighting. We need to be careful in choosing which hills to climb and die on.

NOTES

1. Jason Tish, "Edgewater: Losing the Preservation Argument," Executive Director's Blog, June 10, 2010, at www.madison preservation.org.

2. Marie Rohde, "Milwaukee's Historic Preservation Commission Alderman Robert Bauman Considers Leaving Commission over Marriott Debate," *Daily Reporter*, January 24, 2011.

3. I heard him speak when I was a student. You can find the basic analysis in George F. Kennan, *American Diplomacy, 1900–1950* (Chicago: University of Chicago Press, 1950).

SEVENTEEN

Choosing Our Battles

> When you go up the mountain too often, you will
> eventually encounter the tiger.
>
> —Chinese Proverb

We districtists are human. We can't help but think in terms of
preservation wins and losses in our HPC and on appeal, even
though we are the people's servants. But then they think the
same way, too.

Wins invite confidence. Losses pile on doubt. Yet some
wins cost us future battles, while a loss may conserve our
power for another day. "The side that knows when to fight and
when not to," Sun-Tzu wrote in *The Art of Warfare*, "will take
the victory."

ADVENTURISM

There is a term we can take from the East—well, Moscow anyway. The Kremlin used it to describe ill-advised foreign forays: *adventurism*. We can use it to describe misbegotten efforts on behalf of preservation.

"There are roadways not to be traveled," Sun-Tzu said, "armies not to be attacked, walled cities not to be assaulted"— and rose trellises not to be assailed.

Yep, you heard me right. It lives in lore as "the case of the plastic trellis" from before my time in Annapolis. Resident Bianca Lavies put one up in her garden and was forced to take it down. The case became a cause célèbre as it progressed through the courts on appeal. Local folks still mention it with reference to "hysteria," and that's all that they remember, though in the end the HPC reversed itself before the final courtroom hearing.

A few around here still contend that the drag-'em-to-account action on the trellis should have become our standard practice. But the blowback from that case helped for years to chill the City's will to take all sorts of far more egregious miscreants to task.

PYRRHUS AND FAUBUS

We find it far too easy to let our ordinances choose our battles for us. I know a fellow who blogs incessantly, demanding that our HPC live up to the law's demands. But ordinances are written in the language of empowerment, not command. He quotes text like Holy Scripture. But most everything he quotes actually reads on the order of the HPC "may" do thus and so. I always wonder what part of "may" he doesn't get.

Ordinances invest us with authority, but their authors surely know that power of accomplishment is something different. The link between the two is judgment, about when and how to apply the law and to what effect. Judgment lets us choose most battles. "What it lies in our power to do," wrote Aristotle, "it lies in our power not to do." This has all the tension in it that we expect from politics.

Ideologues and administrative legalists would take power from us by limiting our room for judgment. They would have us choose fights for purity of ideals or jots and tittles in our laws and guidelines. We know them by their heavy breathing over minor affairs. The unwise paths they lead us down may end in

- *Pyrrhic victories*, named for Pyrrhus, king of Epirus, whose costly victory over the Romans at Asculum was his undoing;
- *Faubian defeats*, which I adapt from the talent of former Arkansas governor Orville Faubus for losing in such a way as to take everybody down with him.

Such wins and losses are neither sociable nor formidable. They are plagues on our communities. They weaken our body politic and diminish our effectiveness. We simply cannot afford to let these folks make a sacrifice of good government be the litmus test of our devotion to our duty to protect historic resources.

OUR ELEVENTH COMMANDMENT

The Secretary of the Interior has given us ten standards for historic preservation. Politically, as districtists, we need only one:

**Community support for the historic
district shall be sustained.**

Phrased as a guide to action, it can serve as a law of power conservation:

**Do nothing that may reasonably be avoided
that diminishes the political standing of
preservation in your community.**

When he was president of the National Trust, Richard Moe had this to say: "Obviously, we must always be prepared to fight—and fight hard—to protect . . . historic places . . . But on the other hand, we must avoid the kind of unwarranted rigidity that can cripple our efforts by destroying our credibility and robbing us of public support." He concluded that "we must choose our battles carefully, saving our energy and resources for the fights that really matter."[1]

As commentator William Bennett said of a politician, "He picks fights with the right people. As an old Irishman," he added, "I think that's a good sign." It's prudent, too. And no, you cynics out there, prudence isn't cowardice. It is more on the order of what Rhett said to Scarlett in *Gone with the Wind*. As he handed her a pistol, he told her to shoot anybody who tried to take their horse. "But don't misaim," he said, "and shoot the horse."

Allow me to pose a rhetorical question: if something isn't good politically, can it ever be good for preservation? Picking proper fights is about more than husbanding resources for future battles, as Dick Moe said. The wrong fight weakens us for even routine daily tasks.

We have seen the usefulness of Frank Whitaker's trenchant prodistrict phrase, "The juice is worth the squeeze." In Annapolis, my successor as HPC chair, Sharon Kennedy, has put a twist on it. When confronted with a difficult issue, she says she asks herself, "Is the squeeze worth the juice?"

Gee, I wish I'd thought of that. Now I'm glad to pass it on.

WINNING WITHOUT FIGHTING

There are fights which must be fought. The trick is figuring out which ones. So let's narrow down the field.

Prussian general Karl von Clausewitz helps. In his treatise *On War* he famously stated that war is a continuation of politics by other means—that is, by means other than diplomacy. Diplomacy is sociable and preferable, while war is formidable and uncertain. As Sun-Tzu said, "In war the highest excellence is never having to fight."

That's why we practice politics as diplomacy, which is the search for proximate solutions—that is, accommodations. If we can find a political solution to a conflict then the imperative to fight evaporates.

We should work at all times on shaping a political environment conducive to agreement. I think Sun-Tzu would approve of what I like to call **transformative education**.

NOTE

1. "President's Note," *Preservation*, March–April 2007.

EIGHTEEN

Transformative Education

Return to the fundamentals of politics—sell our story
door to door.

—Chicago mayor Richard J. Daley

To get at what I mean by "transformative education," let's
return to our districting campaign. We started out as preservation advocates, believing in persuasive education. We became
districtists when we ran up against advocacy's political limitations. But others—especially administrative legalists—missed
that lesson.

Preferring to believe that merit won the district, they still
hold fast to advocacy, though with one important difference.
Their postcampaign view of advocacy is one in which *persua-
sion* on behalf of preservation has been replaced by *outreach
education* centered on district law and operations.

INFORMATIVE, NOT TRANSFORMATIVE

Now, I'm a strong believer in outreach education. It is absolutely necessary. Folks have to be informed in a timely fashion about their responsibilities under district law and the penalties for evasion. We owe it both to them and to ourselves.

Dennis Au, City Preservation Officer in Evansville, Indiana, says that "in almost every complaint from a homeowner against the Preservation Commission, it is because the homeowner did not come to us first."[1] If that's because they didn't think to, then outreach education can help drain the swamp of ignorance and prevent casual violations. But even the best outreach education can't work miracles. Folks won't let it.

I'll bet you've seen it, too. Someone from the HPC attends a community forum and makes a presentation. The latest thing is to have online information. So they direct their listeners to the official website. A few folks write it down, maybe on hard-copy handouts. As the meeting adjourns you already sense what happens next. Even if the materials get taken home, they won't be read. If we're lucky they'll get filed away for a later day—*if* they are remembered. As for the website? Most folks just forget it.

And whose fault is this? Not ours, we say. We showed up and talked. Been there, done that, and checked the box on our to-do list. And, like as not, no single attitude has changed.

Why? Because we never even tried. We engaged the community in *informative* rather than *transformative* education. We've restructured no one's thinking about their role in rooted growth and preservation.

TRANSFORMING ATTITUDES

To win folks over, we want to transform their interests and win support for our practices. We'll get the best effect when folks share our objectives. We can't just tell them what they are. They'll think we don't respect them.

We learned this in our campaign, after stalling out with advocacy. Our reset put their interests first and wove them in with ours.

But we did more than that. We couldn't leave them to themselves to work out their response. Left alone, folks will always put themselves before community. We had to involve them publicly in meetings, sociably let's say, to forge community consensus.

That put them among their neighbors. They heard the give and take, and had to take a public stand. All this wrought an internal transformation in many of them. We built community by leading them to a *civic*, not merely a personal, response, adjusting their own interests to harmonize with others.

This we have to do again, especially with newcomers as our district ages. For many of them it will be their first real involvement in community.

Our problem now is that we lack the campaign setting and the advantages of calling district meetings. To win their support for the district and its process, we'll have to work within the HPC and through such forums we can borrow.

IN-REACH EDUCATION

The easiest way is through the HPC. Why not bring them in and familiarize them with our purposes and processes *before* they come before us as applicants? Invite newcomers to a meeting. Welcome them with a "here's what you will see" introduction, say, fifteen minutes before the meeting. Acknowledge them publicly by name so they know they're in the public eye. Then send them on their way after a brief postmeeting follow up Q&A session.

More ambitiously, give them a few applications with annotations pointing to relevant guidelines. Let them follow along—as silent partners, to protect due process—while grappling with the issues, making their own determinations, and getting a feel for how we work with applicants to reach accommodations and serve the greater good. After the session is adjourned, have at least one commissioner conduct a roundtable discussion with them about their experience.

But—and here's a caution—you had better be delivering good government. As essayist and journalist Walter Bagehot once observed in Britain, "The cure for admiring the House of Lords is to go and look at it."

As for closing the disengagement gap with older members of the community, here are just a few suggestions:

- Involve the whole community when you review and update your law, your guidelines, or your practices.
- Press individuals to become involved in long-range planning sessions.
- Constitute an advisory panel to help you keep a weather eye on change.
- Invite them to serve in such other supporting capacities as you may devise that involve some degree of HPC training, such as welcome-wagon personnel, block captains, or observers on behalf of other interest groups.

Get it? Nothing transforms thinking and deepens understanding like participation.

OUTREACH PROGRAMS

Use outreach programs for transformative education. Don't just tell—*show* others in civic forums what we do on the HPC, and involve them.

When James Gibb served as our archaeological consultant in Annapolis, he observed that "most people do not realize the scope of the commissioners' responsibility, the hours of donated service, and the emotional conflicts of critiquing their neighbors' plans. Wearing their shoes might engender a little respect."[2]

Yes, but how? Well, we use in-house mock training sessions to improve our own understanding and performance. Why not do it for them, too? Organizations are always looking for program ideas. Go to your local historical society, Main Street business association, or newcomers group, for example, and offer to do a mock COA review, from soup to nuts, using their own members.

However you do it, make it engaging. Pick sticky topics and devise a couple of credible applications. Instruct them briefly in the relevant law and guidelines. Get them into playing realistic roles as applicants and commissioners, and a few as offering public comments from the floor. Let them deal with the possibilities and limitations of the law, the dilemmas of decision making, and the political imperatives of working to good effect.

Back in our campaign we told our neighbors how the process would work. It helped build confidence. Now you're showing them. Our goal is the same today: to shore up and broaden our political base.

Now, as then, we'll do our best educational work as we answer questions that arise from a *need to know*, driven by their reflection on their obligations and own real interests. This is a far better way of changing thinking than telling them what we think they *ought to know*.

Reach out to difficult property owners. If they don't attend, it puts them on notice of our honorable intention. If they do, it will create a dynamic that either alters their attitudes or inclines others sympathetically to appreciate our effort.

"TELL US" SESSIONS

Another way of being sociable is by inviting various constituencies to HPC administrative meetings for "tell us" consultations. Among these are architects, contractors, landscapers, home-improvement specialists, realtors, and anyone involved in community-development programs.

These folks have a direct interest in our work. We want to ask them two things:

1. How do you think we're doing?
2. What can we do to help you do what you do better?

My experience is that they will appreciate our interest and be frank. This will improve our relationship with them and, indirectly, with those they serve. It will also help us toward better performance as commissioners and staff, keep us abreast of change, and give us insights into the kinds of adjustments we should be making to our law, guidelines, and practices. Then we need to follow through.

This also suggests calling in representative samplings of other groups from time to time, such as recent applicants and even violators. We'll want to know how they found our process: was it accessible and understandable, open, fair, and transparent? We want to hear their gripes, questions, and suggestions, too. The give and take can be transformative and help us appreciate the place of justice in decision making.

KEEPING BRIDGES MENDED

Actors are our hardpan base. We need to keep them close and tighten our connections with other Rooters, too. Personal relationships are transformative. When we befriend folks, we come to share more common views and interests.

It's always a good idea to establish open lines of communication with leaders of other preservation groups, as well as resident and business associations, including the local board of realtors. Asking elected officials for input keeps their interested support, as does periodically attending their meetings at their invitation.

While the HPC chair should be careful about stepping in between staff and their local governmental colleagues, it helps to have at least a nodding acquaintance with folks in municipal departments who are involved in either the district's operation or in public projects in the district.

MEDIA CONTACTS

We are the face of the district in our community. But apart from picturing us through gossip, the public mostly sees us through the press.

The HPC chair should establish a relationship with a key reporter on a basis of mutual trust. Getting good press takes tact. Our interest lies in two places:

1. Getting accurate coverage
2. Influencing the questions reporters ask that shape their stories

Reporters want to do good work. We can help by furnishing deep background information, providing open and timely responses, and explaining the law, process, and technicalities. But we should be careful about privileged information and ex parte discussion of issues that are coming our way or under active consideration.

Helping them be successful works a special kind of magic.

A MATTER OF ATTITUDE

Some of these ideas require a lot of extra work, and not every districting arrangement makes them practical. You are in the best position to know your district and what can work for you. Your state historic preservation office and regional offices of the National Trust may help you find out what folks in other locales are doing.

What's important about these ideas is to think *as if* you'd like to try them out, especially going to the community or bringing people in. If you think this way, you will handle traditional outreach education differently. There, we typically invite questions about procedures. What we also need to do is get folks talking about their attitudes toward districting and their interests in it. We need to find out where our problems lie with them and address them convincingly.

This means being in a constant campaign mode to win them to the district as it ages. It helps if we care whether they understand that the application process is important to the community beyond just satisfying the law and our procedures.

Introductory statements by commission chairs in public hearings typically touch upon the purposes of the HPC. They should also contain a brief sketch of when and why members of the community originally decided it was in their interests to shoulder the personal responsibilities of districting.

ONE-ON-ONE TRANSFORMATIONS

We've suffered a couple of devastating Main Street fires in Annapolis. After the more recent one, the mayor called a next-day meeting. The owner had his people there, and so was I there as HPC chair. When it was my turn to speak, I sensed a tension in the room.

I made a brief, strong case for our community compact and the district process. I affirmed the HPC's settled interest in getting not just good but great contemporary design, to continue our three-century heritage tradition of outstanding architecture. This was, I said, the owner's unparalleled chance to put his stamp upon the district with a structure that would bear his name. I promised we would do all we could within the discretion of the law to expedite rebuilding—even calling special meetings at his behest—while working to accommodate his interests.

Know what happened next? He sat back and said no one had ever explained it to him like that. Goodwill prevailed. Next we worked with him on a first-class project.

The kicker was that outside influences did an end-run around the HPC to produce a shyer and—to *their* minds—more appropriate project plan. You and I might be excused for wondering about the long-run effects this stealth attack generated for the perceived strength and credibility of our district process.

Still, the larger point is that transformative education can be most effective—and is immediately easier—as we handle COAs, especially in such preapplication sessions. Then it's in our district's interests for us to stress opportunities over obligations. When folks want to do something positive, their attitudes toward regulations are transformed. They stop viewing the regulations as "restrictions" and instead elevate them to the status of a "helpful process."

THE SMILE FACTOR

How do you know when the district is working? Remember James Madison on the nature of good government: it conduces to "the happiness of the people." The smile factor is all important.

The only time some HPCs put on a pleasant face is when a meeting is called to order. It's rather as though the chair has taken W. C. Fields seriously: "Smile first thing in the morning and get it over with." One of the nicest comments I ever got was from an applicant who, after a difficult project review, said he appreciated my good humor.

A friendly disposition says you value people and their interests. It might sound corny, but when you're sheltering historic resources from the storm, a smile may be your best umbrella. If folks leave smiling when the hard work is done, you know you've reached them at a deeper level than just an appreciation of the law.

TRANSFORMATIVE LEADERSHIP

Good educators don't just know their stuff. They also know the human landscape they must surmount. To succeed they must be leaders with the right kind of political personality for the job.

Getting the right person in the right place with the right sort of program is all-important. Leadership takes both ability and enthusiasm. If it's not currently available on your HPC, then recruit for it—or seek to make transformative education a part of what your local historical society does in close collaboration.

However it shakes out, this sort of leadership is about more than enforcing our ordinance and insisting on our guidelines. Our most important task lies in sustaining the district ethos we created with our vision at the time of designation.

NOTES

1. Kristen Tucker and Sandra Hoy, "Price of Preservation," *Evansville Living*, March–April 2002, at www.evansvilleliving.com/articles/price-of-preservation.
2. E-mail on file.

NINETEEN

Our Sustaining Vision

The older I get the better I used to be.

—Lee Trevino

What golfer Lee Trevino said is often true of districts, too, when it comes to politics. We played the game early on and won our district's designation. Now some of us have turned our backs upon the game entirely.

A report came out of Traverse City, Michigan, a while ago about a state senator who wanted to give local city councils authority to settle disputes between HPCs and property owners. "I'm a strong supporter of historic preservation," he affirmed, "but there are times that . . . other community needs . . . also must be considered."

A critic claimed that this would "dangerously invite politics into a process designed to save a community's most treasured neighborhoods."[1] But on this evidence alone, politics was there already.

OUR PECULIAR AGE

For all his foresight, I don't remember James Madison, or any of the Founders, ever imagining we'd do such a thing as repudiate politics in a vain attempt to save our districts. Such would have been unthinkable. They mastered politics to better serve the people.

So, to go back to where we started, why is it that folks don't love us more? I think we know the answer. As we've traveled down the road, we've lost our story line: the one about public service.

OUR STORY LINE

The story of our district—the one that we've been working on— is the epic of our compact: the building of community, creating our historic district, and then administering the law to fit the ever-changing needs and interests of our neighbors, as we work with them for rooted growth.

The essence of our tale has been the politics of change. Once we changed the law to get our district designated. It turns out we often haven't been as good at working at the intersection of our district law and change.

Why is that? We have mistaken our authority. Instead of serving people, we've been tempted to bend our power to the service of our preservation interests.

POWER AND PUBLIC SERVICE

When power is uncoupled from the politics of public service, it tempts us to gatekeep historic resources, hew to the details of our law, or take guidance from our principles. Gatekeeping, administrative legalism, ideology: these three distortions of preservation politics show, to borrow columnist Michael Gerson's line, "all the creativity and strategic positioning of a stop sign."

If we let them define the basic ways we think, then indeed our districts are in danger. Folks with crossing interests in their properties, businesses, and lives won't forever tolerate delays and disappointments on our say-so. If we don't succeed with them, we run the risk of district failure.

POLITICS AND VISION

The vision that we need to sustain us isn't some projected future of our liking, or one inherent in our law and guidelines. The vision that we need to preserve our district institutions is right insight into politics.

As well as caring for our heritage, administering the law, and being loyal to principles, we must focus on the three basic imperatives of success that have been with us from the start:

Get power. Keep it. Govern well.

Those who think this way are districtists. The signs that guide them on their way are the perspectives of integral preservation. As capable public servants, they

- Are versed in the precepts and practices of preservation;
- Are familiar with the district's ordinance and guidelines and how the HPC works;
- See the entire community as a set of legitimate competing interests;

- Honor our community compact;
- Define the district's role in terms of contributing to rooted growth;
- Consistently strive to deliver good government;
- Orient their efforts toward mutual accommodation;
- Sustain political support for districting in the community and with public officials.

One characteristic above all else marks them out as leaders. They don't flee from, but instead eagerly embrace, the ambiguity, uncertainty, and inherent tensions that suffuse the politics of decision making.

Edmund Burke, who was Madison's British equal, had high praise for them—for *us*, because by now I trust we all are districtists. "A disposition to preserve and an ability to improve, taken together," he said, "would be my standard of a statesman."

USING POWER WELL

Successful leaders acting as public servants know the uses and abuses of power. In our historic districts, enforcement may *compel* compliance by violators, and it may *deter* others from behaving badly. These things we have to tend to.

But we also shouldn't underestimate the *allure* of power for drawing our neighbors into a culture of compliance. Remember Henry Kissinger on his appeal? The attractiveness of power isn't force. It's the magnetic pull of those who know how to move the world along.

Our neighbors will never love us, but then we didn't ask them to. We campaigned to work through change with them to ensure a living role for heritage in our community. The vision that sustains us now is service through good government that keeps the public's trust.

NOTE

1. Marjory Raymer, "Decisions in Historic Districts May Shift," *Traverse City (MI) Record-Eagle*, October 10, 1999, at www.record-eagle.com.

Selected Glossary

accommodation: The HPC practice of fitting projects to a local ordinance and design guidelines while facilitating approvals of applications for COAs.

Actors: See **Rooters**.

administrative legalism: The tendency to interpret problems arising from COA applications strictly in terms of a preservation ordinance or design guidelines.

Backers: See **Rooters**.

Breakers: See **Makers, Breakers, Takers, Shapers**.

City: Used generically for local governmental authority. Readers may substitute *County* if their districts are in unincorporated areas.

COA: Denotes a *certificate of appropriateness* (or *approval*) issued by an HPC.

community compact: The tacit, consensual agreement for rooted growth among a majority of a district's citizens.

defendable decision making: Arriving at decisions on COA applications that show a care for sustaining political support for district institutions.

defensible decision making: Arriving at decisions on COA applications that are justified by local law and guidelines and show a care for due process.

district institutions: Shorthand for the political superstructure of district operations, including the preservation ordinance, preservation commission, design guidelines, and procedures.

districtist: A person who embraces the perspectives of integral preservation.

facilitating: Working for rooted growth through accommodation.

gatekeeping: Protecting historic resources by resisting change in applications for COAs. *Dispositional gatekeeping* is the tendency to approach COA reviews mainly in these terms.

heritage resources: See **historic resources**.

historic resources: Also called *heritage resources*. Generally, the extant cultural, historical, and architectural legacy of a community. Specifically, the landscapes and features of the built environment identified by a preservation ordinance and design guidelines as triggering HPC overview.

historic preservation commission (HPC): A generic term for an appointive municipal or county board by any name (for example, Historic District Commission, Preservation Landmarks Commission, Architectural Review Board), having primary responsibility for implementing a preservation ordinance.

integral preservation: The distinctive integrative approach to the work of historic districts that seeks both to preserve historic resources and to sustain the political resources underpinning district institutions.

integrity: Denotes wholeness and completeness, rather than honesty. Used to describe historic resources and political support for district institutions.

law: Sometimes used as shorthand to cover both a preservation ordinance and design guidelines.

Makers: See **Makers, Breakers, Takers, Shapers**.

Makers, Breakers, Takers, Shapers: The classification of citizens according to their relationship to an effort to designate a historic district. *Makers* are campaign leaders. *Breakers* are their opponents. *Takers* are those making up their minds. *Shapers* are other opinion makers.

OIMBY Slackers: See **Rooters**, also **OIMBYism**.

OIMBYism: Denotes the attitude of those who engage the historic district process only when their interests are directly involved. Derived from *NIMBYism*'s "not in my backyard" attitude, substituting "only" for "not."

outreach education: Informative educational programs aimed at apprising communities of district processes and owner obligations.

preservation-plus: The district designation campaign strategy that reaches out to emphasize and draw in other interests.

preservation radicals: See **Rotters**.

rooted growth: A term denoting change in which preservation plays an important role.

Rooters: The classification denoting supporters of district institutions. *Actors* take a leading role in the district process. *Backers* support the process. *OIMBY Slackers* are careless in engaging the process.

Rotters: The classification denoting those whose actions subvert district institutions. *Shirkers* evade the district process. *Shredders* are hostile to the process. *Should-Know-Betters*, or *preservation radicals,* support preservation while endangering the district process and its community standing.

second-generation historic district: A district in which a majority of owners have purchased property since district designation.

Shapers: See **Makers, Breakers, Takers, Shapers.**

Shirkers: See **Rotters.**

Shredders: See **Rotters.**

Takers: See **Makers, Breakers, Takers, Shapers.**

transformative education: An approach that emphasizes changing attitudes toward historic districting, beyond *informative* outreach education.

$Index$

political thinking, xii, xiv, 39–40

politics: advocacy and, 18–19;
corruption of, 101; decision
making and, 119–26;
defined, ix; dilemma of, 58–
59; origin of, 3; transcending,
96–99; values and, x–xii,
28, 39–41, 95–101; working
within, xiii–xiv

Polybius, 1

Powell, William, 84

power, 12, 46; contrasted
with authority, 46–47; good
government and, 47, 160–61

power conservation, law of, 142

preservation-plus, 21–22, 27,
96; defined, 165

preservation radicals, 78, 85–86,
95–101

preservationists, types of, 77–81,
85–86

Procrustes, 62

Prolaska, Gary, 58

property rightists, 95–96

property rights, 23, 96n1;
contrasted with political
rights, 23

prudence, as political virtue, 59

Pyrrhus, 141

raison du système, 76–77

Reagan, Ronald, 92

Reap, James K., xiii

Redford, Tim, 29

Rex, Judson, 131

Roosevelt, Theodore, 91

rooted growth, 27–32, 121, 134,
146, 158, 160; defined, 165

Rooters, 77–81, 151; defined,
165; working with, 88–90

Rotters, 81–86, 90–94; defined,
165–66; dealing with, 90–94

rule of law, 92, 120, 123

Rypkema, Donovan, 130

Safire, William, 119

Salt Lake City, Utah, 9

San Angelo, Texas, 28

San Antonio, Texas, viii

San Francisco, California, 28,
29, 53, 69

Saugatuck, Michigan, 9

Sauk City, Wisconsin, 8

Sayers, Dorothy L., 134

Scully, Vin, 108

second-generation historic
district. *See* historic district,
second-generation

Secretary of the Interior's
Standards for Rehabilitation,
36, 52, 90, 97, 142

separability-priority thesis,
59–60

Shafer, Marilyn, 47

Shakespeare, William, 36, 58

Shapers, 21

Wilde, Oscar, 83
Wolfe, Tom, 13, 46
Worthington, Ohio, 48
Wright, St. Clair, 5

Xiaoping, Deng, 105

Zappa, Moon Unit, 37
Zenger, David, 32

About the Author

William E. Schmickle has chaired the Historic Preservation Commission in Annapolis, Maryland. He and his wife, Charlotte, own and operate Flag House Inn in the Annapolis Historic District. Bill was a cofounder of the Oak Ridge Historic District in North Carolina, and he has served as a member of the PreservationNation BrainTrust for the National Trust for Historic Preservation. He is the author of *The Politics of Historic Districts: A Primer for Grassroots Preservation* (AltaMira Press, 2007). A former professor, he has a PhD in politics from Duke University. He writes, speaks, and conducts training workshops on preservation politics (www.preservationpolitics.com).